The

MASTER

MOTIVATOR

The MASTER MOTIVATOR

Secrets of Inspiring Leadership

MARK VICTOR HANSEN
JOE BATTEN

JAICO PUBLISHING HOUSE
Ahmedabad Bangalore Bhopal Bhubaneswar Chennai
Delhi Hyderabad Kolkata Lucknow Mumbai

Published by Jaico Publishing House
A-2, Jash Chambers, Sir Phirozshah Mehta Road
Fort, Mumbai - 400 001
jaicopub@jaicobooks.com
www.jaicobooks.com

Published in arrangement with
Enterprise Center
Health Communications Inc.
3201 S.W. 15th Street
Deerfield Beach, FL 33442-8124, USA

THE MASTER MOTIVATOR
ISBN 978-81-8495-720-4

First Jaico Impression: 2015

Printed by
Repro India Limited
Plot No. 50/2, T.T.C. MIDC Industrial Area
Mahape, Navi Mumbai - 400 710

CONTENTS

FOREWORD

It is not often that I have accepted the opportunity to write the foreword to a book. The invitation to be part of *The Master Motivator*, however, was one I could not turn down because of the two parties involved: Joe Batten and Mark Victor Hansen.

Both Joe and Mark have stood the test of time. For the past 20 to 30 years, they have continually honed their craft and stirred the giftings in their students. Their ideas and enthusiasm have also inspired me.

In this insightful book, Joe and Mark skillfully present the fundamentals for becoming a great leader in both business and family, as well as for becoming the best you can be personally. They lead you to the keys of success. The great thing about success is that it is not complicated, nor is it magical or mysterious. It is a simple process: Success is merely the natural consequence of consistently applying proven fundamentals to your life. In *The Master Motivator,* Joe and Mark have masterfully taken the seemingly complex and made it simple and doable for the reader.

The search of Joe and Mark's protagonist, Doug Sanchez, for the fundamentals to both personal and business success begins with the good fortune of finding a mentor. (I've always subscribed to the powerful Biblical phrase, "If you search, you will find".) With the guidance of this mentor, Doug begins the process of becoming a student. The wise mentor weaves into his conversations with Doug the powerful truths and principles that must be acted on to become a Master Motivator. The mentor introduces Doug to the fundamentals of success: the power of dreams and goals; the importance of personal development and self-discovery; the value of helping others; and the necessity of utilizing your own unique strengths. I believe that you, the reader, will glean a crystal-clear vision of these truths as the mentor teaches these principles step by step. Most important, you will be inspired to take action and begin this new process for yourself.

For those who have already achieved a level of success, this book will be a reminder of the many ideas you originally feasted on but that you now may overlook in your daily habits. We all need daily mid-course corrections; it is part of the whole success equation.

So for the new as well as the seasoned student, this is a book you will want to highlight key points in, make notes about, and periodically go back and review. And as you continue your upward move toward personal and business success, share these principles with others so you, too, can be a Master Motivator.

Jim Rohn, C.P.A.E.
Author of The Five Major Pieces to the Life Puzzle
and The Seasons of Life

PREFACE

If you truly wish to gain insights and skills in one-on-one motivation and become a Master Motivator, read on. . . .

Our story traces the incredible growth of Doug Sanchez as he progresses from "adequacy" to excellence, from tragedy to triumph, as he learns to motivate himself and others. He dares to become all he can be, and he motivates his team members and family and friends to do the same. Discover how he made optimum contributions and obtained unlimited results.

All true motivation is self-motivation to action. Acquiring the skills of self-motivation to action and making it a habit is not easy, but it is doable. Every one of us has the potential inside. Sometimes it takes a Master Motivator to unlock that potential in us. The motivational mentoring presented in Doug's story has examples of self-motivation pitfalls and failures as well as successes. The goal is to grow, become stronger and move forward.

The Mentor encountered herein has no name because it is important that the reader's perception of him be internalized and personalized. We sincerely hope that every reader will conscientiously complete all of the exercises and assignments and find a mentor who inspires him or her to become a fully developed human being. Great individual changes will spontaneously occur.

Perhaps the finest gift you can give another person is the gift of an excellent and stretching expectation, based on a never-ending search for that person's present and potential strengths.

If you truly want to become all you can be, read this book again and again. Learn, master, own, utilize and share these principles and ideas. Will you do it? We're cheering for you.

ACKNOWLEDGMENTS

It is a major challenge to even attempt to acknowledge some of the debt we owe so many. When Leonard Hudson joined Joe Batten in 1958 and Hal Batten and Jim Swab came aboard in 1959, Batten, Batten, Hudson & Swab became a company dedicated to helping individuals and organizations *become all they can be.* Years later Joe gave this phrase to the U.S. Army, but it has remained our fundamental purpose for being and serving.

Our evolving team has included many who have gone on to enormous success in their own companies, and that is good.

Here are just a few to whom Joe owes much. They include

Mary Roelofs and Melva Edwards, whose functions as his executive assistants have been invaluable. Others are Art Bauer, John Wade, Hector Sanchez, Dennis Murphy, Bob Johns, Judy Porter, Bob Gappa, Sharon Ward, Joyce Sullivan, Shirley Winner, Diane Hockett, Frank Russell, Barbara Wickham and Bettie Youngs.

Those who contributed directly to this book are Jared Van Horn, Chris Hudson, Bill Pearce, Norm Fleming, Robert Pugh, Leonard Hudson, of course, and Bradford Pugh. Joe's gratitude to his wife, Jean, and daughters Gail and Wendy simply cannot be expressed in words.

Other clients and colleagues who have profoundly influenced Joe include Ross Perot, Konosuke Matsushita, Berkley Bedell, George Morrisey, Zig Ziglar, Robert Randolph, Don Kirkpatrick, Norman Vincent Peale and Donald Alstadt.

Mark Victor Hansen is especially thankful to Cavett Robert, whose motivational tape, "Are You the Cause or Are You the Effect?" saved his life after he went bankrupt in 1974. Mark let Cavett's tape mentor him through 287 listenings. It redirected Mark and inspired him to get up and go forward with his life.

Mark appreciates his wife, Patty, for her unending love, support, devotion, thinking and complete helpfulness at every level of his life.

Jack Canfield has been a total mastermind partner, friend and confidant.

Dr. Buckminster Fuller was Mark's intellectual mentor, teacher and friend who inspired him to think comprehensively and to discover how to make the world work for 100 percent of humanity.

Annually, Mark chooses at least one new mentor in an area in which he wants to grow, develop and express proficiency. Some recent mentors Mark wants to thank include Dr. Jeffrey Lant, Dr. Jean Houston, Joel Weldon, Jay Abraham and Bob Allen.

INTRODUCTION

Motivation: Getting some. Giving some. Being inspired. Inspiring others. Leading self. Leading others. Everything is about motivation, isn't it? Your happiness and well-being; your productivity, achievement, success and self-esteem: all of these are integrally connected to motivation. From cradle to grave, we're all deeply involved in the art of inspiring ourselves and others. Consider how imperative it is that you be a master motivator in the most crucial tasks of your life:

- Can you motivate your colleagues and staff to be as passionate about the goals of your company as you are?

Can you inspire them to strive to turn in a peak performance, giving their best zestfully, not grudgingly? Can you encourage them to act conscientiously and ethically, adhering to a code of conduct that increases their joy, satisfaction and self-esteem while fostering a dynamic and synergistic environment? Can you urge them to seek self-fulfillment, but not at the risk of the company or its members? *It takes a master motivator.*

- Can you convince that extraordinary special someone to venture into a lifetime commitment with you? Can you instill a desire to be loyal, supportive, monogamous? Can you bring that person to care for *your* well-being as much as her own? Can you earn her respect and create a foundation for her to hold you in the highest esteem? Can you encourage him to value sovereignty, but at the same time think in terms of *we*—placing the well-being of the union over his individual pursuits? Can you persuade your partner to value your differences and see them as positive and enlarging, allowing each individual and the union the fullest expression of talent, happiness and satisfaction? *It takes a master motivator.*
- Can you give your children the greatest gift of all: the security of knowing they can always count on your skill and protection? Can you instill in them the commitment to give their all to anything they undertake? Can you help your infant to let go of the side of the crib and take those first few steps without assistance, or reassure your toddler that it's okay to let go of the side of the pool and begin to swim toward you? *It takes a master motivator.*

- Can you inspire within a young child the sense of confidence to leave the safe nest of home and, with positive expectations, look forward to the challenge of a classroom of judging peers and a new, unknown teacher? Can you convince your child to do her homework when she is too tired, is unsure of how to do it or lacks interest in the subject matter? Can you stimulate a child to commit to the rigors of learning, from a first math class to learning to play the piano, and to see value in it? Can you instruct children to be the best they can be personally, yet show them the importance of sacrificing the *me* for the *we* of the team? Can you persuade a child to keep his room, and himself, orderly? *It takes a master motivator.*
- Can you coax your adolescent into considering the advantages of packing a parachute when he'd prefer to soar the skies of life without one? Can you convince her to honor her responsibility to the family when instead she seeks autonomy? Can you entice him to spend time with you, when he'd prefer your car keys? Can you show her how to support the goals of the group—to fit in—yet be true to herself? Can you impress on him the importance of adhering to his values even in the face of adversity? Of coming home at curfew? Of getting up in the morning on his own? Can you teach him to hold sacred another's right to choose and let it rule out over his own raging hormones? Can you imbue her with the strength to be personally and socially responsible? Can you infuse him with the confidence to pursue purposeful goals? *It takes a master motivator.*

- Can you inspire your grown child to look forward to the challenge of leaving home, starting college, beginning a job or career, working purposefully, starting a family of her own and living a principle-centered life? *It takes a master motivator.*
- And perhaps most important, can you encourage yourself to be the best you can be? Have you taken responsibility for your life, recognizing that you are the instrument of your own performance? Do you take the time regularly to provide self-leadership by drawing upon the sources that inspire and uplift you? Do you open your mind to new experiences and regularly reevaluate your assumptions? Do you read broadly, exposing yourself to great minds? Can you inspire in yourself the continuing commitment to goals—peace of mind, relationship harmony, learning and education, status and respect, leisure time, health, wellness and fitness, financial security, work and career success—that give meaning to life? *It takes a master motivator.*

Motivating yourself and others is a big order to fill, but it is necessary if vitality is your goal. It's difficult to live a meaning-*full* and purpose-*full* life without mastering the skills to motivate self and others. Likewise, it's unlikely that a successful company that is competitive in its field—one that has managed to recruit and retain vibrant, high-producing, high-achieving, success-oriented, stimulating and happy people—would have such motivated employees in the absence of a knowledgeable leader, a master at motivation. Motivation is what differentiates talkers from doers, dreamers from achievers, a good department from a dynamic one, families where related people simply live together from those that are healthy and happy. But the path from wanting results to getting them is paved with more than mere intentions: whether motivating self or others, it takes exemplary motivational *skills* to be successful.

Presidents, parents, department heads, supervisors, college deans, pastors, foremen, heads of agencies—all are engaged in getting things done with, and through, people. Each must be skilled at the four basic tasks that make any group or organization run efficiently and effectively: planning, organizing, controlling and motivating. Of these, motivating is the most sensitive and vital: it is interdependent on each of the other functions. Planning is the setting of goals and objectives, and the development of the map that shows how these goals and objectives are to be accomplished. Organizing is the effective integration of resources—people, capital and equipment—in order to accomplish established goals. Controlling is evaluating results and adjusting actions that have caused outcomes that deviate from expectations. Motivating determines the level of performance of people, which, in turn, influences how effectively the group or organizational goals will be met. In other words, leaders must be master motivators. Failure to motivate causes dissension in the workplace, which is reflected in collective resistance, adversarialism, a deep lingering malaise and other chronic problems.

Ideas on the art of motivation have changed considerably over the years. The history and development of modern motivational theory is an interesting journey, especially the *human relations* movement that originated in the 1930s. This was a radical departure from the early 1900s, when Frederick Winslow Taylor and other theorists believed that the best way to increase productivity was to improve the techniques or methods used by workers; this spawned the *scientific management* movement. Time and motion studies were used to analyze work tasks to improve performance; jobs were reorganized with efficiency in mind. The function of the leader was to enforce performance criteria to meet the organization's goals. The leader was concerned with the needs of the organization; employees were expected to adjust to management.

But the conclusions drawn by the efficiency experts at the Western Electric Company in Hawthorne, Illinois, in 1924 changed all that. Their study became one of the most exciting and important research projects ever undertaken in the field of motivational research. In their attempts to find the ideal mix of physical conditions, working hours and working methods that would stimulate workers to produce at maximum capacity, an incredible truth about human motivation was revealed: people need to feel important. This finding came about quite by accident. Efficiency experts set out to test the hypothesis that increased illumination would result in higher worker productivity. To prove their theory, they subjected a *test group* to working under varying degrees of light, while a *control group* worked under normal illumination in the plant. They assumed that as lighting power increased, the productivity of the test group would also increase; meanwhile, the control group, under normal unvarying illumination, would remain constant. Instead, they found that while under increased illumination the productivity of the test group did go up as expected, the productivity of the control group also went up without any increase in light. Perplexed, they called in Elton Mayo of the Harvard Graduate School of Business Administration to help them explore the surprising test results.

Mayo and his team noted that when workers were given improved work conditions such as scheduled rest periods, company lunches and shorter work weeks, their productivity went up as expected. When these benefits were taken away, however, not only did the productivity of this group continue to go up, it jumped to a new all-time high. The explanation was simple: the attention lavished upon the employees made them feel like an important part of the company, even after the material benefits were removed. Being thought of as a team—as participating members of a congenial, cohesive work group—elicited feelings of affiliation, competence and achievement. Over the next few years, this phenomenon was tested again and again in a number of different settings. The results were the same: obviously human affairs were too important to overlook. And so it was that the *human relations* movement was born.

One of the best cases made for motivation as a vital leadership function is found in the work of Harvard's William James. James found that employees could consistently produce at 80 to 90 percent of their ability *if highly motivated.* Moreover, if motivation was low, performance suffered to the same degree as caused by low ability. Obviously, motivation was an extremely important function of management. An important next question was: *What* motivates people?

A good number of other researchers expanded and enlarged our ideas about not only the nature of motivation, but of what serves as motivators. For example, Mayo's work paved the way for the development of the now classic "Theory X-Theory Y" by Douglas McGregor. McGregor knew that traditional organizations, with their centralized decision-making, superior-subordinate pyramid and external control of work, were based upon assumptions about human nature and human motivation. Theory X assumes that most people prefer to be directed, want safety, are not interested in assuming responsibility and are motivated by money, fringe benefits and the threat of punishment. Because people are basically unreliable, irresponsible, immature, and need structure, control and close supervision, managers would therefore need to focus their efforts on an attempt to structure, control and closely supervise their employees. Luckily, McGregor knew that this view accounted for a limited number of workers; many people are capable of mature behavior and want to demonstrate this capability. This led to Theory Y, the tenets being that people could be self-directed and creative *if* properly motivated. Under this assumption, management's role was to unleash this potential; if properly motivated, people could achieve their own goals best by directing their efforts toward accomplishing organizational goals.

Along came Abraham Maslow with his theory based on a hierarchical structure of needs such as safety, security, self-esteem and self-actualization. Maslow's work was useful in that it identified needs or motives, but it was Frederick Herzberg's work that provided us with insight into the goals and incentives that satisfy these needs. Herzberg fathered the *motivation-hygiene theory* (in today's time more commonly called the motivation-maintenance theory), an insight into human nature, motives and needs. Basically, Herzberg set out to collect data on job attitudes from which assumptions about human behavior could be made. He concluded that people have two different categories of needs that are separate and independent of each other and affect behavior in different ways: when people felt dissatisfied with their jobs, they were concerned about the *environment* in which they were working; when they felt good about their *jobs*, this was due to the work itself. The first set of needs was called hygiene or maintenance—hygiene because they describe the environment and serve to prevent disaffection; maintenance because they have to continue to be satisfied. The second group was called motivators since they are effective in motivating people to superior performance. Interestingly enough, hygiene-maintenance factors eliminate dissatisfaction and work restriction, but do little to motivate individuals to superior performance. Motivators (recognition for accomplishment, challenging work, increased responsibility, growth and development), on the other hand, produce feelings of achievement and result in an increase of productivity. These findings opened the floodgates for those studying the subject, eventually leading to the work of Paul Hersey and Ken Blanchard and their theory of *situational leadership*, a model that examined the interplay among the amount of guidance and direction a leader gives, the amount of relationship behavior a leader gives, and workers' levels of maturity. Theory, then, serves us well in that it gives us a framework for understanding human needs: for example, Maslow is helpful in identifying needs or motives and Herzberg provides us with insights into the goals and incentives that tend to satisfy these needs.

It's both easy and interesting to observe the art of motivation in practice. I have held positions in the classroom and the boardroom—I've worked with students and with Fortune 500 managers; I've worked over the years in business, industry and education; I've taught university master's and doctoral-level courses and started a company of my own. From these experiences, I know firsthand that some theories are outdated for the nature of our world and workforce today, and that some theories never were good for organizations or the people within them. I have been in companies where ill-fated managers foolishly spent their time growing a bigger and better brand of carrot to entice employees to reach these managers' goals. Spending energy in this way only creates within others a misaligned ability to do what it takes to garner the carrots. A master motivator, on the other hand, empowers others to create for themselves a desire to produce, achieve, excel; only then will there be an advance in profit, productivity, growth and positive change.

Consider how important this is in our world today. The shift from a manufacturing society to an information society and from physical labor to mind-work as the dominant employee activity; the onset of a technological society magnified and accelerated by continual scientific and technological breakthroughs; the emergence of a global economy, itself characterized by rapid change: all of these demand a new mindset and new skills at every level in the workforce. A workplace characterized by innovation, change, speed, newness, competitiveness, diversity, stress and pressure requires a high degree of personal autonomy, self-reliance, independent judgment, self-management, personal responsibility and self-direction from all employees. Such an environment places demands on our emotional energies and psychological resources, but it is enormously important for adapting to an increasingly complex and competitive workworld. Leading others in this brave new workplace takes leaders who don't demand, but encourage; who don't push, but direct. It requires leaders who are able to rally the troops and bring forth their best—without burning them out.

The case for being a master motivator is an easy one to build; the question then becomes: *How does one become a master motivator?* The key to effective management of self or of others is not a technique or tool; *it is intrinsic.* Motivating begins with introspection, begins with self-examination or, as my friend Stephen Covey says, must begin "from the inside out." Self-understanding is the key. The master motivator begins by first examining his or her own motives, needs and desires. Master motivators are fairly easy to recognize. Generally, they are high-achievers who have a style of zest, zeal and gusto, and an ongoing richness and fullness to their lives—lives, I might add, that are literally crowded with balance. But even more, the master motivator commits not only to his own growth, but to the growth of others as well. The master motivator has a following of admirers (young and old) who can attest to the many doors of opportunities that were opened for them. Just as the master motivator knows how to create and travel the path to fullness, he knows how to imbue it in others.

The authors of this book are two such men: two master motivators. Styles as different as night and day, both men are effective because they understand precisely how to engage people in passion. They know how to lead with passion, knowing full well that motivation involves (1) engaging others in the desire for personal excellence, (2) showing others they are a valuable part of the team and (3) stimulating the dream machine in order to share in the abundance that is a natural outcome when these other principles are put in place.

I know Joe D. Batten and Mark Victor Hansen. How do these men measure up? Are they themselves master motivators? Many years ago I was an educator and was named my state's Teacher of the Year. As part of the honor, the morning after receiving the award I gave a presentation to a Chamber of Commerce. After I finished my talk, I saw a distinguished gentleman approaching me. He smiled and said, "Some day, I'd like you to come to work for me. Here's my card. Take the time to learn about *our* company, and when you're interested, come and see me." Joe D. Batten—president and CEO of Batten, Batten, Hudson & Swab (BBH&S), a management and consulting firm providing service to Fortune 500 companies—managed in those few words to open my mind to opportunities I'd never considered before. But that wasn't the last I heard of this master motivator. Several years later I completed a doctoral dissertation in management and leadership. A professor suggested I examine the characteristics of three of the most viable companies in the state, concentrating on their leaders. Somehow I wasn't surprised to see the name Joe D. Batten again.

Years passed. I developed an interest in knowing how business, industry and education were alike and how they differed. By this time I'd held positions of leadership in education and governmental affairs; the dynamics of the business world intrigued me. Wanting to flex my mental muscles, I put on my dark blue suit and knocked at BBH&S one day. Here was a company with a master motivator, a man who led as though he had no rank. This leader depended on the quality of his ideas, expressed through his example. His was a company staffed with high-energy women and men who were fit, sharp and passionate for their goals—and what big goals they were. Here, mission statements were lived out in the everyday context of business. Here was a master motivator who expected excellence and knew how to inspire it in his staff. At BBH&S my muscles got a real workout. I signed, and stayed on for a number of years. It remains, to date, one of the most dynamic and growth-inspiring experiences of my 25-year career.

Not all master motivators come in the same mold. Mark Victor Hansen is a master motivator of a different nature. Mark is motivated by the art of the sale, with joy being the only acceptable route in getting there. I met Mark some 16 years ago as I accepted an award for doing something or other. While I may not remember the particular award, I'm not as vague about the man who presented it. Here was an energy, a force, a dynamo who—though he knew me only from my work—presented me to the audience with words and actions that were as leading, loving and honorable as any I've ever heard. His goal that day was his usual one: get to know someone, make them your friend, support them, ask that they support you. And have fun doing it. Is it any wonder that this master motivator masterminded the idea of a collection of stories gathered from friends and colleagues around the world, and turned the book, *Chicken Soup for the Soul* (co-edited with friend Jack Canfield), and its companion, *A 2nd Helping of Chicken Soup for the Soul,* into *New York Times* bestsellers?

And best of all, Mark is having so much fun just being alive that people around him share in that joy, knowing that he's as happy being in their presence as they are to be in his. If you find yourself vacationing on a beach some day, don't be surprised if Mark comes up to you and, in the course of a conversation, sells you the rocks and seashells on the beach, masterminds a plan for mass distribution and convinces you that your new business is going to be the most fun you're every going to have. Mark is hopelessly the greatest salesman in the world, having fun playing out his life. His needs and goals are simple: he wants to discover how to make the world work for 100 percent of humanity. And he intends to involve you in the process.

Joe and Mark: different in their styles, but alike in their passion and ability to motivate. These two master motivators understand precisely how to instill in people the desire for personal excellence. And that's what this book is about. In this book you'll meet and accompany Doug Sanchez on a most extraordinary journey of growth, from being an ordinary good guy to becoming a master motivator. This is a book about translating the quest for personal and professional excellence into action, and developing and sharing the abundance that results when people are motivated to be the best they can be.

Bettie B. Youngs, Ph.D., Ed.D.
Author of Values from the Heartland

1

DOUG REMEMBERS. . .

The room was filled with a special kind of electricity. The air pulsated with anticipation and energy. This was a happening. Everyone tingled with excitement. Leaders, spouses and the staff of the Profitable Products Company had gathered for the gala Annual Awards Dinner. It felt like Oscar night. Expectant whispers filled the air as everyone speculated about who would win.

Dazzling awards sparkled under halogen spotlights. They were for Sales SuperStar, Best Business-Builder, Safety Now and Peak Producer. Most coveted of all was the new award called The Master Motivator.

The applause got progressively more thunderous as the corporation's stars cascaded across the stage, receiving recognition, praise, applause and increasingly more coveted trophies for their extraordinary respective performances. As the evening progressed, the men and women of Profitable Products were treated to the sight of many outstanding people receiving appreciation for their hard work, dedication and exceptional skills.

Tension peaked as the time for the final award approached. The Master Motivator award would be presented personally to the winner by the CEO, Brad Boulder.

Brad rose to pay tribute to the winner of the award. He paused, smiled and let the tension expand. Then he said, "It makes my heart sing to present this award for the first time. Our future as a company depends completely on the one-on-one motivational skills and practices of every one of our people.

"We've all been wowed as we watched our winner grow, change and enjoy and experience constant and never-ending improvement. He has become a Master Motivator! It's a real joy to present this year's award to a splendid person. And . . . his name is Doug Sanchez!"

Doug's countenance shone like an angel's as he effortlessly stepped forward to accept his well-earned trophy. The audience burst into a rousing standing ovation. Everyone had come to love, honor, respect, admire and appreciate Doug's phenomenal transformation.

As Doug and his wife, Marya, drove home after the dinner, they were ecstatic, and Marya said, "Doug, this has been the best year of our lives. It flew by—365 days seem like 365 seconds. You started out like a caterpillar. Your attitudes and energy level were low. Then you entered a magical chrysalis and learned new ideas, principles and attitudes. You've emerged as a high-flying, resplendently beautiful butterfly that radiates love, joy, kindness, wisdom and high self-worth. The kids and I love what's happening to you and us. You're a better businessman, leader, father and husband. I'm so proud of you. Congratulations and thank you, my love."

Marya leaned back, her expression thoughtful. Then she smiled.

"By the way, did you notice The Mentor sitting back in a corner? He was really beaming when you were walked up to receive the award."

Doug nodded, grinning. A few minutes later, he pulled the car into the driveway. Doug and Marya walked hand-in-hand into their comfortable home. Doug stretched luxuriously in his recliner and loosened his tie. After a few minutes of happy silence between them, Doug leaned forward. "Marya, it does seem hard to believe. I remember so clearly how it all started. . . ."

2

SELF-DISCOVERY

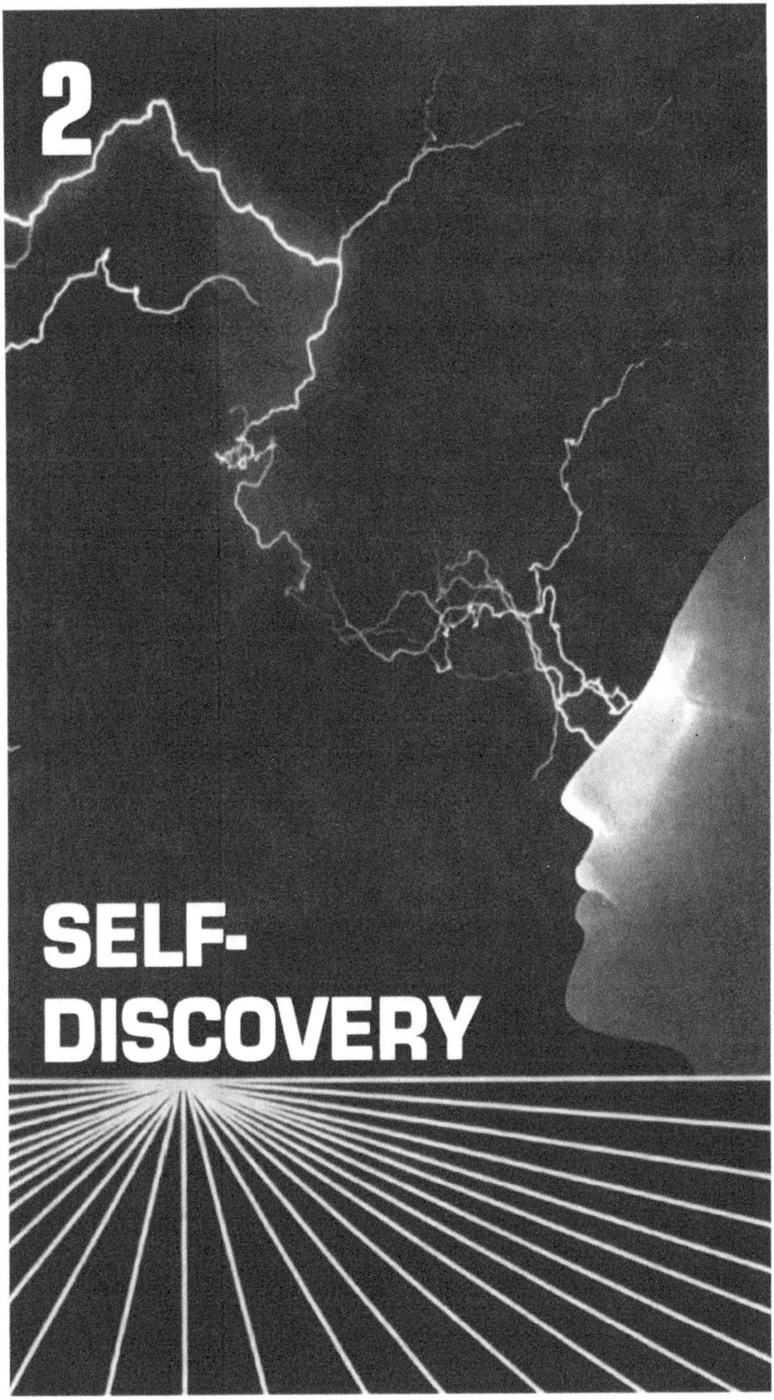

I don't seem to be going anywhere, Doug thought, either on or off the job. "A floating generality" seemed to best describe the way he felt. In his mid-30s, he also didn't know whether he was a particularly good father or husband. He loved his wife, Marya, but didn't feel as close to her as he thought he should. He didn't communicate to her any of his dreams or goals . . . perhaps because he wasn't sure what they were. His son, Dan, and daughter, Sandi, were "good kids," but there didn't seem to be any real purpose or direction guiding the family. The same feeling applied to his job.

Shortly after this self-appraisal, Mark Jackson talked with him about his annual performance review. "Doug," he said, "I seem to sense great potential in you if you could only learn to more effectively motivate yourself and others. You've got good experience, a good education and no real handicaps, but you're not growing, improving and developing; and unless you do, we can't promote you. You run your department fine, I guess, but I sense your team lacks a rudder, a real sense of direction.

"With your permission, I'm going to arrange for you to have some sessions with a man I just call The Mentor. Will you meet with him tomorrow in his office? I'd appreciate it."

Doug shrugged. "I'm willing to try." As he departed, he felt as if his mind and soul were smiling and singing. As he talked to himself, his positive feelings increased.

"Wow! I've got great potential," Doug said to himself. "Mark sees more in me than I see in myself. No one ever told me that before. If he believes I can achieve, I can."

When Doug walked into The Mentor's office the next morning, he didn't know what to expect. He had some vague trepidations and uneasiness. He had heard through the grapevine that The Mentor found the hidden greatness in his mentees and nurtured them until they bloomed, thrived and flourished. Doug hoped he deserved such attention because he certainly desired new possibilities.

The Mentor started out with seemingly countless questions. Questions of all kinds. He appeared sincerely interested in how Doug felt. What were his hopes, his dreams, his fears, his frustrations? The Mentor's body language radiated caring and he actively listened. His eyes patiently absorbed Doug's every nuance and movement with each answer. Doug found it easy to open up under this skillful past-, present- and future-revealing questioning. The Mentor wanted to see where Doug's dreams would take him. Finally, he came to the core of Doug's dream. "I guess I'd like more than anything else to be able to positively influence and lead people. I'd like to get really, really good at it. I honestly believe that then I could be a real success."

Smiling, The Mentor said "Great, Doug; let's take a look at a total strategy for becoming a fine motivator."

The Mentor looked Doug squarely in the eyes. "First you have to motivate yourself. To do that, you need to understand Charles Tremendous Jones's classic line: 'You'll be the same person you are now—five years from now, except for the people you meet, books you read, and tapes you listen to.' And to that we add, the movies you watch. The best shortcut to success is to have a great and inspiring teacher, a mentor. A mentor is a personal coach who challenges, inspires and stimulates you to manifest your full potential. I'll be your first major mentor. After that you will discover the old cliché is true: 'When the student is ready, the teacher (mentor) appears.' You'll have many more mentors in the future; and as you do, you'll keep the cycle glowing, going and growing by being a mentor to other deserving mentees.

"Next, I've prepared a must-read booklist for you. [*See* Must-Read Books *at end of this book.*] The great ideas in these 12 books will motivate you from the inside out, so that you can motivate others positively and effectively. Make it a new discipline to read these books at least a half-hour per day, preferably at the beginning of your day. Get up 30 minutes earlier. Note that I've written a sentence about what I expect you to find in each book. We will discuss them in depth. You need to take active mental ownership of these concepts. To do that, follow the recommendations in each book and implement them as you read them. Re-read the books and discuss your new awakenings, insights and understandings with your wife, children, colleagues and team. Re-stating what you've learned will motivate you and those you lead. En route to work, start listening exclusively to educational, inspirational and motivational tapes. Every motivator needs to be motivated. In principle, take all your waste time and make it reading time."

He flipped on his overhead projector, illuminating a transparency entitled, "Blueprint for One-on-One Motivation."

The Mentor continued, "You can see we've started our discussion of self-discovery via books, tapes and me. Now let's just skim lightly over all eight steps in the blueprint." After reviewing the eight steps, he said, "Okay, throughout our meetings you'll get homework to do, but first let's review a few things. . . ."

Figure 1. Blueprint for One-on-One Motivation

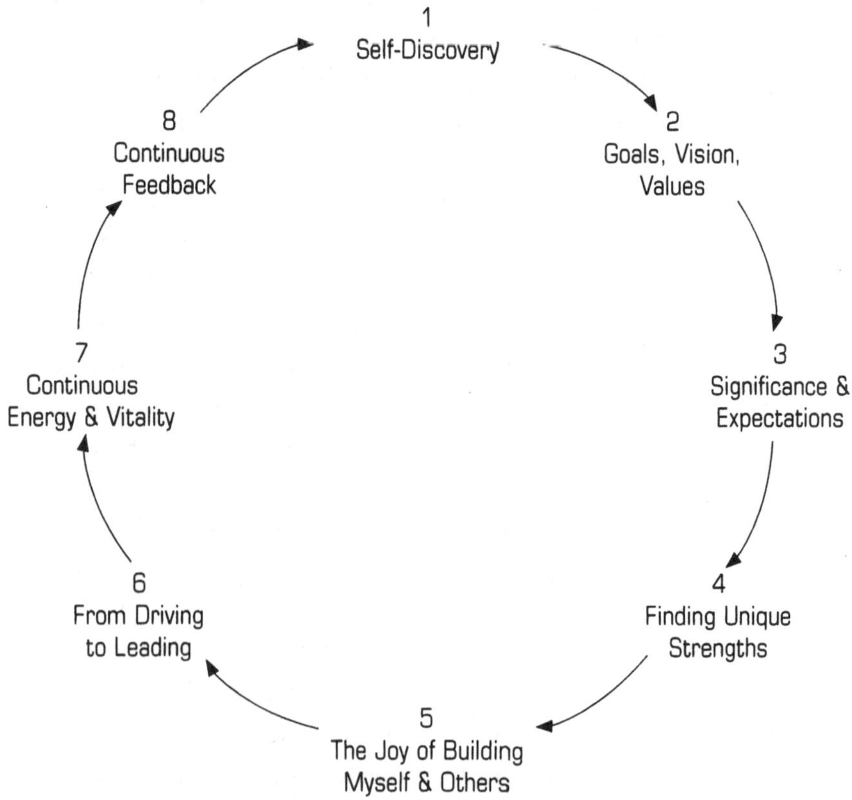

1. I will learn more about my strengths and possibilities.
2. I will live and work with purpose and direction.
3. I will ensure my motivatees feel real and goal-oriented.
4. I will help my motivatees discover strengths and possibilities.
5. I will ensure that my motivatees discover the joy of building and creating.
6. I will lead and lift rather than push and diminish others.
7. I will endeavor to help my colleagues become all they can be.
8. I will continuously evaluate the progress of my motivatees.

Wants and Desires

"Needs are of course very important," The Mentor said. "Your wants and desires, however, will condition and affect what you feel you need. Your wants and desires are the basis for your *motives.* The real meaning of motivation or motive action requires that you develop a crystal-clear set of motives and then the 'ation' or 'action' needed to achieve and fulfill the motives." [*See* Glossary of Motivational Terms.]

Doug shook his head in awe. "So that's what motivation *really* is!" He was amazed at how The Mentor could take a simple word that Doug took at face value and give it a whole new spin. Doug would never think of the word motivation in the same offhand way again.

Fears and Defenses

"There's more," said The Mentor. "Your fears and defenses are the greatest barriers to freeing up your potential.

"You need to clearly perceive and understand what you're afraid of in every dimension of your life. You see, when we walk around with our invisible defenses up, we simply cannot grow, create, care or relate to others. And relating to others is what motive-action is all about."

Doug was thoughtful. "I'm beginning to realize there's a lot about myself I need to learn. I need to start looking inward more."

The Mentor smiled. "That's right, Doug, and I'm sure you will."

"I'm a Good Person!"

The Mentor led Doug through some more questions and found, as he had suspected, that Doug was primarily aware of his weaknesses rather than his strengths. In short, Doug saw himself as a very "common and ordinary" person—a definition many people internalize.

The Mentor knew Doug must begin to see, perceive and relish the good things in himself, but his background and conditioning had not equipped him to do so. The Mentor asked Doug to affirm out loud: "I am enough!" "I am a good person!" "I am somebody!" "I make a difference!" At first, Doug felt self-conscious and embarrassed. But this slowly gave way to the insight that verbalizing his goodness was self-empowering. After repeating these affirmations, Doug started feeling better and better.

Getting Ready to Dare

The Mentor asked Doug if he cared enough about his job, his family and himself to dare enough to complete some specific action steps on the road to self-discovery. By now Doug was enthused about the whole process, and he agreed to complete some specific action steps before their next meeting. He did not think of them as "homework." He thought of the exercises as "lifework."

Specific Action Steps

- Write down the five things you most want and desire in life.

____

____

____

____

____

- Write down the five things you most fear in life.

____

____

____

____

____

- Write down ten things about you that are *good.*

____

____

____

____

____

____

____

____

____

____

	YES	NO
• I see each of the people in my department as a bundle of strength.	____	____
• Starting immediately, I am going to expect the best from each member of my team.	____	____
• Starting right now, I am going to try catching my team members doing something right.	____	____
• I will begin searching for qualities in me to love.	____	____
• I will begin searching for qualities in others to love.	____	____
• I will begin visualizing myself as a *good* person at all times—I will make the word "good" a basic part of my vocabulary.	____	____

Current Focus Inventory

WHAT I'M FOR (Need and Desires)	WHAT I'M AGAINST (Fears and Defenses)

Self-Discovery Inventory

MY GREATEST STRENGTHS	WHAT I'M AGAINST WEAKNESSES

Love begins when a person feels another person's need to be as important as his own.

—Harry Stack Sullivan

3

GOALS, VISION AND VALUES

As Doug began meeting regularly with The Mentor, the eight steps in the Blueprint for One-on-One Motivation [Figure 1] started coming alive. He began applying each step to each person who reported to him on the job. As Doug studied, experimented and came to truly understand all that follows in this book, he began making noticeable progress with each team member. He did not always succeed, but he kept working at it and kept discussing progress with The Mentor. As he focused on motivating each person, he moved from helping each discover himself or herself to helping the men and women on his team truly understand what led and pulled them.

Looking to the Rainbow

One evening, as Marya straightened up the family room, she sang a few lines from *Finian's Rainbow*, "Looking to the rainbow to follow your dreams. Follow the fellow who follows a dream." Doug, who had been helping her, stopped, exclaiming excitedly, "That really fits with the Blueprint. The rainbows in our lives are the *visions* we reach for, the *goals* that provide the *motives* for our motive-action."

Doug thought about how the rainbow visualization could be used with each person on his team. He started to ask, listen and hear on the job in order to better aid his team members to think through and write down their own visions and goals.

He began realizing that the total value of each person is the sum of his or her individual values, and that the total value of his department was the sum of the values thought, taught and practiced there. He resolved to appreciate the values of each team member.

Vulnerability Means Invincibility

Gradually Doug realized that the people on his team would grow stronger, faster and be more vulnerable and open to change if he could consistently try to "catch them doing something *right*." The Mentor said, "The more earned praise you give, the better you and the other person feel."

He was amazed to discover that this power-filled motivational tool—earned praise—could be practiced anywhere, any time, if one simply cared enough. Perhaps even more exciting was the pleasure he derived from doing so. Doug was not only rewarding his people, he was receiving satisfaction in return.

Doug was also impressed with the concept behind "vulnerability means invincibility." As The Mentor explained, if a person is guarded and invulnerable, that person withers and experiences no growth. But if that person is open and vulnerable, truth and candor are let in, like beacons of light illuminating a path of growth.

Caring, Sharing and Daring

Doug sat bolt upright in one of his sessions with The Mentor when he heard him say, "Do you *care* enough to *share* enough to *dare* enough to be *aware* enough of the goals and possibilities of others, wherever you are?"

A Code of Values

"That's dynamite," said Doug. "I'm going to discuss this with Marya and Dan and Sandi. This just might be a good start on the Family Mission Statement we've been talking about. If I get confident and sensitive enough to do this at all times, I have a feeling life's going to be much richer."

The Mentor nodded. "Being aware of the goals and visions of those around you adds texture to your life . . . and your family's life."

Doug grinned at The Mentor. "Yes, and you always manage to say things so succinctly. You really motivated me with that one."

In response to Doug's request for assistance in formulating some goals, visions and values, The Mentor suggested that he complete the following to start:

Specific Action Steps

	YES	NO
• I see each of the people in my department as a bundle of strength.	____	____
• Do you lead as though you had no rank, as though you had to depend on the quality of your ideas expressed through your example?	____	____
• Will you think through and write down your own macro goal for your life?	____	____

	YES	NO
• Will you think through and write down your major goal for each year?	____	____
• Will you make sure your colleagues always know in advance what you expect from them in the way of conduct and performance on the job?	____	____
• Will you commit to setting the right example for your team by your own actions in all things?	____	____

Four steps to achievement:
Plan purposefully—Prepare prayerfully—
Proceed positively—Pursue persistently

—WILLIAM A. WARD

4
SIGNIFIANCE
AND
EXPECTATIONS

One evening, Sandi sat at the kitchen table doing her homework while Doug started dinner. She put down her pen and stared out the window for a minute or two. Then she asked, "Dad, how can I know I'm real—that I really count?" Doug had grown so steadily in his role as motivator that by now he didn't hesitate. "Sandi, do you think you help the people in your life at school and here in the family feel better about themselves?"

Sandi thought a bit and then said, "Yes, I do." Doug stopped what he was doing and sat down at the table opposite her. He smiled lovingly and said, "Then you're *real—you count.* And the more you enrich the lives of others, the more you'll enrich your own, and the more real you'll become." Sandi beamed with pride. "Thanks, Dad."

Later, Doug saw how this same truth applied to his own team members and he vowed that he'd do all he could to help them to also feel *real* and to *count.*

We Grow When We Stretch

A muscle only becomes stronger and more effective if it is stretched and exercised. It's the last repetition we do, after we can't do any more, that causes the most growth. The muscle's growth stops when it is given too much rest. Real motivation is impossible unless the person is steadily and consistently reaching for goals that require stretch and effort.

Doug knew one of his people, Laura Bosco, could and should be more productive. Laura did just enough to keep her job, but no more. Doug reviewed each step in the Blueprint for One-on-One Motivation and decided the answer was to *expect* more from Laura. Doug proceeded to do this by positively inspiring Laura about what he expected from her, and sharing with her a new and omni-attractive vision of Laura as she could become.

Laura's performance changed very little. Doug was puzzled. Then it occurred to him he had *told* Laura what he expected of her, instead of *asking* her. Doug had expected more before he had applied the steps in Chapters 1 and 2.

Doug had continued trying to catch Laura doing something *wrong* rather than trying to catch her doing something *right.* When he started catching Laura doing something right, Laura's performance started changing. Laura kept doing more and more right. The idea was profoundly simple and simply profound. Doug's motivational skills were growing, but there was so much to learn!

We Must Be Before We Can Do

As Doug reviewed these first steps, he realized that helping Laura determine what she wanted to *be* would result in helping her improve the quality of what she *did.*

Doug asked Laura all the questions suggested in Chapters 2 and 3 and really *listened.* He asked, listened and heard. It was then that he noticed Laura's level of vitality and commitment began improving. Laura was beginning to feel *significant!* This significance translated to better job performance.

At the same time Doug discovered that asking got better results than telling, he also began seeing the power of clear expectations. Telling is pushing and driving. It diminishes others. It is being *directive!* Asking is empowering and lifting. It is *expecting* rather than *directing.* Increasingly Doug understood that "we become what we expect."

The Mentor suggested that Doug put the following message in visible parts of his work area and on the wall of his home office:

> Perhaps the finest gift one can give others is the gift of excellent and stretching expectations, based on a never-ending search for their present and potential strengths.

Then The Mentor asked Doug to carefully think about and complete the following:

Specific Action Steps

	YES	NO
• Will you make every effort to frequently say: "I value and appreciate you and your possibilities?"	___	___

YES NO

WHY? ______________________________________

____

____

____

WHY NOT? ______________________________________

____

____

____

- Do you agree: "A relentless focus on strengths and clear, stretching expectations enhances the true feelings of significance, dignity, worth and individuality of the motivatee."? ____ ____

WHY? ______________________________________

____

____

____

WHY NOT? ______________________________________

____

____

____

- Do you believe: "To know what is clearly expected of one is to tap the wellsprings of true motivation"? ____ ____

WHY? ______________________________

____

____

____

WHY NOT? ______________________________

____

____

____

• Think carefully and complete the following:

My most important expectations of me are:

____

____

____

____

____

____

____

My most important expectations of my motivatees are:

____

____

____

____

____

____

____

____

____

In a Nutshell

Develop a clear and complete system of expectations in order to identify, evoke and use the strengths of all resources in the organization—the most important of which is people.

Look for strengths in people, not weaknesses: good, not evil. Most of us find what we search for.

—Anonymous

5

FINDING UNIQUE STRENGTHS

The more Doug recognized, acknowledged and accepted his strengths, the more they grew. He took little steps at first, gaining confidence, self-esteem and self-love. Gradually, he witnessed his enormous inner strength, power and talent. His inner self was infinitely able, capable and loving once he discovered it. Everywhere he looked, he now saw opportunity and possibility. Life was becoming a full-time adventure!

The Reality of You and of Me

The more he could see, feel and moderately and progressively test his newfound strengths and inner resources, the more they grew. Best of all, once he owned them, he could nurture and coach them in his team members. The more he expected of himself, the more he was able to expect from those around him. As Doug's feelings of significance as a person increased, he contributed more to the strengths and significance of others. He was making an important difference and everyone he touched, talked to and teamed up with was now doing the same or more. Doug felt enormous breakthroughs.

Launch a Never-Ending Search

One by one, Doug met with each of his team members and encouraged each to begin building his or her own "strength notebook." Team members were asked to write down every strength they could think of about themselves and then add a new one each week for a year. When a person thinks about his or her strengths, those strengths grow, quickly, like beautiful roses blooming in April. The Mentor told Doug that some people continue to keep this notebook for many years. The rewards are both phenomenal and omni-beneficial. Doug had been hearing a lot about something called "reinventing" himself and his company, and about organizations known as "learning corporations." Doug was reinventing himself and his team. He was learning and creating his own learning corporation as a now-online just-in-time university.

Doug read that the university of the future was the corporation. Now he knew it. His mind was ablaze with life. He felt unstoppable. Daily he input a half-hour of inspirational, educational and motivational tapes while driving to work. He loved listening to the likes of Mark Victor Hansen, Joe Batten, Tony Robbins, Jim Rohn, Zig Ziglar, Danielle Kennedy and others. Nightly just before going to sleep, he was reading Napoleon Hill, James Allen, Jack Canfield and others, learning principles, processes and procedures that he knew all the greats used.

He loved reading and rereading *Self-Reliance* by Emerson. He was modeling in his sleep and implementing in his work. He likened his mind and spirit to a body-builder who had been training for six months and suddenly had burned off the baby fat and now had a hard, lean, attractive body. His new resolve, self-sufficiency and self-respect were gaining him prominence, proficiency and popularity in all aspects of his life. It was happening fast and felt great.

He discussed this in detail with The Mentor. The Mentor knowingly and proudly smiled. Doug got it: Every organization could and should be a learning organization! Every excellent organization is continuously reinventing itself. Every superstar organization is involved in constant and never-ending improvement. Improvement that starts with one individual.

Doug could now see that every individual is one who can make a difference. He loved the idea. He wanted everyone to be a part of a learning organization. One night he dreamed that the real purpose of life was learning, and it was his job to inspire everyone he met to get the message and then mentor another. Doug now understood that within three decades, it was possible that 100 percent of humanity could become 100 percent successful economically, physically, financially and socially one person at a time—thanks exclusively to mentoring, which is communication and collaboration.

Every company, division, department or section has its own P-Pyramid: Purpose, Programs, Processes, Policies and Philosophy; and each person must be pervasively saturated with the commitment to learning and continually inventing himself or herself and that organization.

The enlightened pursuit of total quality functioning, fed by the never-ending search for strengths and ever clearer and more stretching expectations, fuels this total reinventing effort.

Figure 2. P-Pyramid

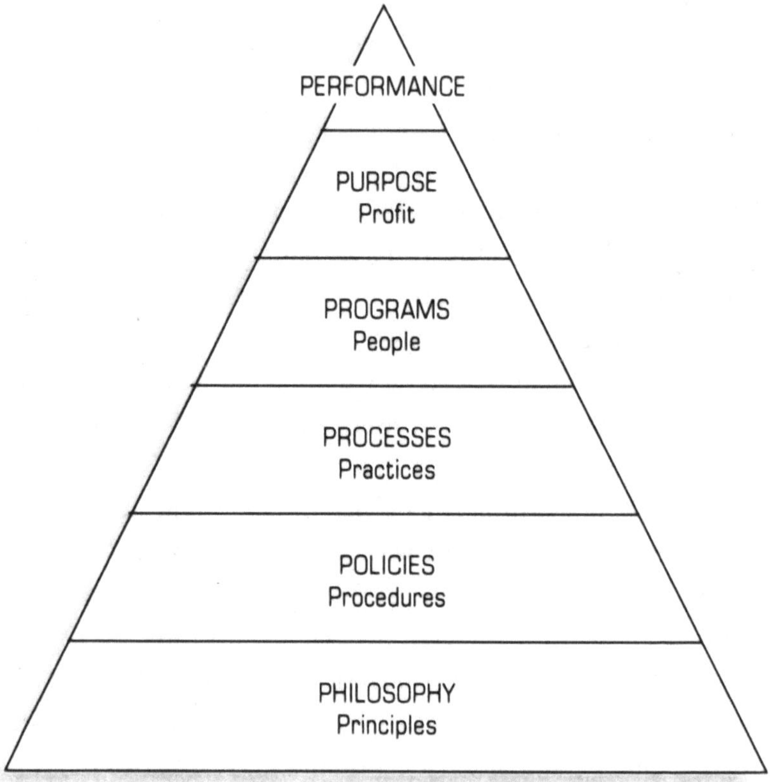

The Tool Kit on Your Shoulders

The Mentor inspired Doug to see that each team member carried a comprehensive tool kit on his or her shoulders. It was in plain sight, but generally invisible to its owner. Doug read Russell Conwell's great classic, *Acres of Diamonds.* Again he was energized by the concepts within. The book's main theme was that each person has infinite assets. Once discovered, these assets can benefit that person and the whole world. Doug's new mission was to wake up and inspire others to discover their acres of diamonds. This was a major challenge, and Doug found he was up to it.

Together with the team members, he placed a sign in a prominent spot, visible throughout the department. It read:

> Our strengths are
> our tools.

Doug's Search for New Tools

As he actively searched for new ways to develop and motivate each team member, Doug asked The Mentor if he had some prepared materials to use in this motivational process. The Mentor gave him an article he had written and suggested that Doug give copies to each team member and then have individual and group discussions about self-change.

Challenges for Self-Change

Our individual and collective fortunes will rise or fall in direct proportion to the strength and resilience of our attitudes. Excellence results from exceeding ourselves, from becoming all we can be, from daring to dream and then living the dream. We have the dream (idea) and then the dream has us.

All too few of us experience those moments of real excellence called epiphany. Why all the mediocrity? Why all the pinched and pallid faces in the mirror? Because of all the poor attitudes. Attitudes are *everything!* We can learn to tell our feelings how to feel. Each of us can wake up every day saying, "I feel good and I will feel even better." As this is said with feeling and belief, these words *become* our individual truth. We consciously and unconsciously start feeling consistently good.

Our attitudes are at the core of our being. They condition our biological anatomy, the activation of our brain cells, our choice of nutrition and exercise, and *ergo*, the condition of our bodies, minds and spirits. Attitudes condition our relationships with others. They are truly the agents of change and arbiters of the quality of our lives.

When we are performing at the peak of our powers, when we are experiencing excellence, we are acting out positive attitudes, passions and dreams. The lift and pull of a transcendent dream is at the core of all human progress. Pasteur, Curie, Schweitzer, Watson, Peale, Emerson, Perot, Beethoven, Einstein, Marriott, Iacocca, Fuller, Gates, Spielberg, Turner, Disney and others who profoundly influenced their time were all focused and centered on a dream. They were not distracted or defeated by self-doubt.

Passion and passivity mark the difference between people whose lives burn with the fires of great ideas and people who putter around aimlessly.

I want to issue a specific challenge to people who are committed not only to achieving excellence as executives, but also to living a full and zestful life—what Dr. Abe Maslow, the father of positive self-image psychology, called a "fully functioning, no-limit, self-actualizing individual." In spiritual circles, this concept would be defined as striving for spiritual self-mastery or avatar. *Therefore, I challenge you to dare to be all you can be!*

Every day, affirm: "I am a genius, and I apply my genius," an affirmation written by Dr. Paul Bragg. Your one trillion brain cells work like a robot at your command. Command them to think, "I am a genius as a parent, and I apply my parenting genius." (We are the first generation to think such bold family-improving thoughts.)

"I am a genius as a visionary leader, and I apply my leadership genius." (As you outpicture this vibrant vision, your strengths and leadership skills will grow and manifest daily.)

"I am a financial genius, and I profitably apply my financial genius."

"I am a genius at learning, and I apply my learning genius." Marva Collins is an extraordinary educator who takes Chicago ghetto children, under-achievers and non-achievers and finds the genius in them. She will not let them fail. When these children are four years old, Collins starts helping them read and understand Ralph Waldo Emerson's *Self-Reliance* and Shakespeare's *Merchant of Venice*. She says there is genius in everyone. She mentors it out.

The Mentor's 16 Dares

From this article, The Mentor issued 16 "dares." Did Doug (and his team members) . . .

1. *Dare to live passionately?* Dare to be all you can be. This challenge is even more significant today. From it, we have the other dares.
2. *Dare to dream big and to put time and energy into making that dream a reality?* He asked Doug to daily devote some time to developing his dream of what and who he could become. The Mentor said, "There

is no other individual like you on earth. Seven billion people have lived on this planet, and all were and are different. Think about your possibilities, your strengths, the wonder of you and set a self-fulfilling prophecy into motion."

3. *Dare to build a fine, fit body?* No one lives in neutral; we build or destroy with everything we think, say and do. Few of us would deliberately destroy anything, and yet we often destroy our own potential and fall far short of our dreams by not keeping our bodies in top condition. The Mentor pointed to the newest research that shows we need to be aerobically fit and exercise five to six days a week. Covert Bailey, author of *Fit or Fat,* says we need to walk, swim, run, jump rope, cross-country ski (downhill is not aerobic), play singles tennis or be on the Nordic Track or Fitness stepper, 20 minutes or more until we break a sweat, while being able to talk simultaneously conversationally without being out of breath. The Mentor advised Doug (and Doug in turn told his team members) that after a health professional had checked the soundness of his body, he needed to cautiously build up to 20 minutes of exercise each and every day.
4. *Dare to nourish the mind and spirit?* The Mentor repeated the adage that we become what we eat. To expand that idea, he said, we could add that we become what we absorb. If we absorb not only nutritious (go heaviest on fresh organic fruits, vegetables, legumes, herbs and grains) foods but also fine art, literature, music and other enriching material, we

nourish the mind and spirit as well as the body. If we give love, understanding and affirmation to others in generous quantities, we absorb the riches of those relationships. We become a great deal more. Our capacities to lead and love become infinitely greater.

5. *Dare to shun rigidity and keep an open, inquisitive mind?* "I want your mind to thrive and grow resilient, fit and tough (not hard) as you set goals that require you to stretch, to keep reaching day after day," said The Mentor. "Just as a physical muscle is strengthened by overcoming resistance and stress, so also is the mind conditioned and strengthened. Dare to develop a tough mind and a tender heart." Joe Batten gave Martin Luther King the idea and substance for his known sermon, "A Tough Mind and A Tender Heart." It is reproduced as Chapter 1 in this book, *Strength to Love.*
6. *Dare to expect the best from yourself and other people?* Dare to look searchingly for virtues, talents and strengths in all people. We commonly get what we expect; the times can be as bad or as good as we expect them to be. Our expectations produce our experiences. Doug liked this one especially.
7. *Dare to find something to love in every person?* Love fuels all fitness, all growth, all creativity, all excitement and all richness. The Mentor pointed out that any fool can hate and belittle others. Wise people learn to love and lift others. Research has verified that love can literally heal many diseases of the body, including cancer in some cases.

8. *Dare to set goals that are too big for you and then to grow and stretch to fulfill them?* Effort and stretch lead to both physical and professional development. Stretching efforts are best motivated and sustained by committing to challenging goals and by exceeding our previous performance. Start by setting goals. The Mentor wanted Doug to ultimately write a 50-year plan, as Walt Disney had. Disney died in 1966, yet Disney Parks in Florida, Japan and France have opened, and his company has gone from making five movies a year to 60 feature films a year—all because he knew what he wanted, wrote it down, storyboarded his goals (on display at Club 31 at his Anaheim park) and masterminded with his team so that his legacy could be carried out. "I dare you to write up a 50-year plan," The Mentor smiled.
9. *Dare to fill your heart and home with faith, hope, love and gratitude?* While people have immediate and ongoing needs for security, recognition, significance, opportunity and belonging, their most important and fundamental needs are for faith, hope, love and gratitude. Heartfelt gratitude and non-chemically induced depression cannot coexist. Genuine gratitude heals and helps create a state of happiness and emotional fitness. It's the finest kind of mental hygiene. Make it a point to express gratitude to at least one person every day. Doug found that this wholesome practice grows and grows until, like The Mentor, he lived in an almost perpetual state of joy and bliss.

10. *Dare to live with a sense of wonder?* This may be the nearest thing to a full state of grace. For anyone who wants to increase effectiveness, this is an important challenge, The Mentor said. Nothing can deaden or abort progress more quickly than getting stuck in the rut of "comfort zone." A sense of wonder, too, may be killed by cynicism, sarcasm, negativism or determinism. On the other hand, it may be cultivated by reaching, searching and confronting your possibilities. This works particularly well in an atmosphere of real learning where you have dialogue and collaboration with your mentor.
11. *Dare to live life vulnerably?* This requires and creates courage, commitment and confidence. Emotionally open and vulnerable people grow and change. They seek and relish innovation and challenge. They stay vitally alive until their last breath. Invulnerable or 'safe' people become rigid in mind and weak in body and spirit. They seek to avoid all obstacles, oblivious to the fact that too much comfort can lead to the ultimate state of rigidity known as rigor mortis. Doug was already living vulnerably, and vowed to keep it up.
12. *Dare to write down 200 victories in your life since your birth?* "At first you may be unable to think of that many victories, but please persist until you have recorded 200. It can be done. Over the years, I have encouraged countless executives to do this and have witnessed the payoffs in more positive self-concepts. If you truly desire to be a peak performer, a peak motivator, you will work at displacing all losing thoughts

and replacing them with winning thoughts." The Mentor's voice radiated excitement and confidence.

"I'll start my list tonight!" Doug replied.

13. *Dare to create and build a personal-strength notebook?* "Write down every single strength you can think of that you currently possess, and then resolve to write down one additional strength each week. People who continue to do this year after year increase in fitness, strength, self-confidence and richness. In a sense, you are the sum of your strengths; they are the best tools you possess. Get in touch with them!"

    Doug, again, was thinking more and more in terms of strengths. Writing them down only served to reinforce them.

14. *Dare to build on your strengths?* "Remember that your weaknesses manifest what you are not. A weakness is only an absence of a strength or an insufficiently developed strength. Thus, we can't build on them; we must build on strengths.

    "Find a mastermind partner who is strong where you are weak. Your mere association with him or her will strengthen you," said The Mentor.

    Doug thought this even applied to his marriage. Marya had strengths where Doug was sometimes weak. She balanced the family budget better than he. She was more gracious in social settings and a better conversationalist. Doug, on the other hand, was stronger in a crisis and better at motivating the kids in their schoolwork.

15. *Dare to be a "go-giver"?* Another expression from The

Mentor: The go-getter ultimately gets got. Any selfish amateur can! The more you give, the more you get. It is a great cybernetic truth. For starters, here are four things to give: inspiration, aspiration, dedication and perspiration toward a worthwhile destination.

16. *Dare to compete with your own goals and possibilities?* The amateur competes with others. The professional competes with his or her own goals and possibilities. The goal is to outperform yourself: Children crawl, walk, run and then jump. Most of us cease actively growing between the 20th and 30th year of life.

"I dare you to grow forever," The Mentor challenged. Cavett Robert wisely says, "If you cease to grow, you begin to die." Doug loved reading the parable of *Jonathan Livingston Seagull* because he discovered that one only competes with oneself.

All true champions do this. Coach Vince Lombardi taught that whenever a player *re*acted to a member of the opposing team, he lost precious split seconds and, therefore, his advantage. He believed strongly that the "pro" *pro*acts, which causes the "amateur" to *re*act.

There is a growing need for managers and leaders of substance and style who understand that personal and organizational excellence are really all about, by and for *people*. Dare to exceed and move beyond the stereotypes. Dare to exceed yourself, to become the ultimate you. *Do you care enough?*

The 16 "dares" provided fuel for some challenging and thought-provoking discussions. Doug's department was beginning to become a subject for comment and discussion throughout the company.

Specific Action Steps

With The Mentor's counsel, Doug developed a 18-point inventory to assess the motivational effectiveness of his leadership. Each team member was requested to complete all 19 of these questions and reflect on them daily.

Do the traits, talents and possibilities of my team members include:

	YES	NO
• A high level of mental, physical and spiritual energy?	____	____
• Willingness to be bold, articulate and vulnerable?	____	____
• Commitment to *expecting* rather than *directing?*	____	____
• Style that favors pulling rather than pushing?	____	____
• Passion rather than passivity?	____	____
• Being supervisor-*led* rather than supervisor-*driven?*	____	____
• Willingness to figuratively "walk in front of the flock"?	____	____
• Zest for growth, change and renewal?	____	____

	YES	NO
• Personal example that empowers, stretches and motivates others?	____	____
• The giving of *earned* praise and personal empowerment?	____	____
• Commitment to transcendent vision, values, missions and *goals?*	____	____
• Working to replace the negative "driving" G-forces of the past? *(See* Glossary of Motivational Terms *in back of book.)*	____	____
• Plugging into the positive "motivating" G-forces of the future?	____	____
• Knowing that consistently applied truth and candor *set you free?*	____	____
• Believing that integrity and strength have exactly the same meaning?	____	____
• Translating values into actions?	____	____
• Savoring innovation, creativity and constant change?	____	____
• Placing a premium on a *team* composed of empowered, motivated people at all times?	____	____

Each of us has a deep
need for feeling significant as a
person, and such feelings are
enhanced
by clear, stretching expectations
and an empowering focus
on strengths.

---

*People ask the difference between
a leader and a boss. The leader works
in the open, and the boss is covert.
The leader* leads *and
the boss* drives.

—Theodore Roosevelt

6

THE JOY OF BUILDING OTHERS

Doug was glowing as he moved from success to success, from achievement to achievement. He felt more empowered and empowering by the day. Marya was ecstatic for Doug's mounting achievements and their ever-improving relationship. She said, "The Mentor got you wound tight, darling. Dan and Sandi are seeing and feeling the changes, too, and they're delighted. What's happening?"

Doug smiled. "What I'm enjoying most," he said, "is my new relationship with *each individual person* in my department. I'm particularly committed to motivating and mentoring Laura Bosco, or to be precise, to *helping Laura motivate herself.* It all comes from within, you see, and it's just a downright pleasure to make sure I *teach* and *exemplify* each of the eight steps in the Blueprint for One-on-One Motivation.

"You see, if I can do a truly *excellent* job of motivating Laura, or helping and leading her to motivate herself, she can replace me and I'll be able to accept a promotion when it comes. And I *know* that's going to happen.

"As I become more, I can help others become more. When I grow, my world and our world improves. What's amazing is I've discovered that it all begins with me."

Marya looked thoughtful. "Can you give me an example of what you're doing with Laura and the others?"

"Sure I can—easily," smiled Doug, reaching for his wife's phone note pad, and flipping to the first blank page. He was so happy that she shared his enthusiasm for all he was learning. This shared excitement was deepening their partnership.

The G.R.O.W.T.H. Acronym

Doug sketched out the following six steps:

Goals, vision, mission and dreams
Realistic assessment of strengths
Openness and vulnerability
Wonder, a sense of
Tough-minded expectations
Hope

"Can you see how these six steps all mesh beautifully with everything else The Mentor is teaching me? I'm trying to pass them on to my people, Laura in particular.

"Goals provide lift, pull and focus, and they stimulate. They motivate! They are the core of motivation. Inspired goals get inspired results."

Marya smiled, her expression encouraging Doug to go on.

"The realistic assessment of strengths helps individuals gain some real insights into what they are capable of and instills a great yearning to *become all they can be.* It motivates!

"Openness and vulnerability to new challenges and possibilities help insure growing strength, confidence and mental toughness. All these concepts motivate!

"Wonder, which is cultivated constantly, helps to dissolve and blow away cynicism, negativism and demotivation. It motivates!"

"Now I really see how you motivate," Marya said. "Your voice, your body language—you embody energy."

"Exactly. These principles are never-ending. Tough-minded expectations in all dimensions of a person's life help insure that he or she is always reaching, stretching and achieving rather than simply reacting to the pressure of push and drive. They motivate!

"Hope, as The Mentor says, is the universal nourishment for all growth, all richness, all motivation."

We Find Ourselves by Losing Ourselves

Laura Bosco and Doug met regularly for motivational discussions. Each time they reviewed progress and growth, new questions arose. At one point Laura said, "Doug, I notice you've become such a giver. Isn't it possible to give *too* much?"

"Possibly," replied Doug, "but I deeply believe that the more one gives of self—that is, information, dedication, perspiration, counsel, coaching and expectations—the more the giver grows. Gandhi said, 'You will *find* yourself by *losing* yourself in *service* to your fellow man, your country and your God!'

"The foundation for quality friendship lies in the belief, 'When I meet the needs of other people, my needs will be met.' Friendship, therefore, is an extension of the natural laws of life."

Doug then recited an apt poem.

What you give, you get
What you send out, comes back
What you sow, you reap.

As she internalized these ideas, Laura's level of motivation climbed steadily.

Ask, Listen and Hear

The Mentor recommended positive, active, interested listening.

The Mentor sounded grave as he counseled Doug to be aware that all of the motivational breakthroughs he was achieving could be canceled or negated almost immediately if he lapsed into *negative listening,* which means simply waiting until the other person has stopped speaking and then saying what you were going to say anyhow. Other forms of negative listening occur when one provides an answer *without knowing the question!* Another insidious way to destroy good communication is to *finish the other person's sentence* for him or her out loud.

Doug was finding this to be a highly valuable practice as he continued growing as a spouse and parent.

Wants, Needs and Possibilities

Doug still tended to suspect that *telling* rather than *asking* was justified sometimes.

To become capable of asking,
listening and truly hearing requires
a consistent and caring application
of all that has been presented
in the book so far.

Perhaps the most potent and
tested counsel for all who truly want to
motivate others, or help them achieve
their own motive-action,
is the following. Think about it again
and again and again.

*Ask, listen and hear
in order to determine
their wants, needs and possibilities.*

The Mentor shook his head, "No, Doug, it all depends on how you do it. You may shout, rant and bellow and get compliance only. But when you ask, *mean it!* Keep experimenting and you'll convince yourself. Telling diminishes others. Asking enhances and empowers others."

The Mentor's Prescription: ASK!

- If you don't know, ask!
- If you are unsatisfied, ask!
- If you want to lead rather than push or follow, ask!
- If you want to consummate a persuasive objective, ask!
- If you are tempted to respond to a situation with anger and a directive statement, ask!
- If you desire to communicate (shared meaning and shared understanding) rather than simply engage in dialogue, ask!
- When bored with directives and declarative statements, ask!
- When beset by confusion, ask!
- When you encounter hostility and passive resistance, ask!
- When you expect good things from life, ask!

Doug liked these ideas so much that he taped them to his desktop next to his phone and read them each time he was on hold, for 30 days. The results were nothing short of miraculous. Laura tried, again it worked. Laura got Sam to do it. The Mentor was getting reflected glory for his mentee and mentee's mentees.

Originally, when Doug heard The Mentor stress the importance of learning his motivatees' needs, wants, fears and desires, he was somewhat puzzled about how to determine this. Now he understood that asking, listening and truly actively hearing with his inner ear were skills that could be honed throughout a lifetime.

Laura Bosco helped him see that three of the most powerful addages in the history of humankind were worded in the following order:

Ask and it will be given you,
Seek and you will find,
Knock and it will open unto you.

Empowering and Reinforcing

The Mentor told Doug that to empower is to create and foster relationships in which people understand their *significance, possibilities* and *strengths.* People who are empowered have a clear understanding of their authority, responsibility, accountability and valued role on the team, and they have autonomy that is symbiotic with others. You get *power* by giving *power.*

Positive reinforcement and the tough-minded term *build on strengths* mean one and the same. One definition of reinforcement is "to strengthen with new force." It is crucial to understand that the only synergistic way communication can be built is through the combined strengths of the individuals involved. A weakness is only the absence of a strength, or an insufficiently developed strength. Strong, effective communication cannot be created from absences. Each of us is defined or profiled by our strengths. Our strengths alone comprise what we *are.* Thus, we must begin looking (and, in fact, never stop looking) for strengths in ourselves. Only then are we able to perceive, relate to and further build on the strengths of another person.

Positive reinforcement can be, and often is, only a fatuous phrase unless it derives its nourishment from self-confidence. Real self-confidence can be fully functional only in relation to other people. An organization must do all it can to create a work climate or culture in which people are respected for *who* they are and recognized for their contributions to a job well done.

Empowerment and reinforcement are central to *all* positive motivation!

"Okay," Doug said, "I can sure see why reinforcement and empowerment help one become a Master Motivator. But you've also made it clear that the best motivators have an entire lifestyle of achievement and happiness. Can you give me a few specific traits for the guidance of men and women who want to lead *real* lives?"

"You betcha!" said The Mentor as he walked over to a flip chart. He then wrote out specific, clear steps to take for Doug and others interested in motivating.

Specific Action Steps

Master Motivators must:

- Care much

  Why ____________________

  How ____________________

  When ____________________

- Dare much

  Why ____________________

  How ____________________

  When ____________________

- Share much

  Why ____________________

  How ____________________

  When ____________________

- Stretch much

  Why ____________________

  How ____________________

  When ____________________

- Expect much

  Why ____________________

  How ____________________

  When ____________________

- Give much

  Why ____________________

How ______________________________

When ______________________________

- Live much

Why ______________________________

How ______________________________

When ______________________________

- Love much

Why ______________________________

How ______________________________

When ______________________________

- Grow much

Why ______________________________

How ______________________________

When ______________________________

- Experiment much

Why ______________________________

How ______________________________

When ______________________________

- Seek challenges and obstacles

Why ______________________________

How ______________________________

When ______________________________

- Have a sense of wonder

Why ______________________________

How ______________________________

When ______________________________

• Have a specific program of physical, mental and spiritual fitness

Why ______________________________

How ______________________________

When ______________________________

• Constantly pursue a greater awareness of their own strengths

Why ______________________________

How ______________________________

When ______________________________

• Constantly pursue new acknowledgment of the strengths of others

Why ______________________________

How ______________________________

When ______________________________

• Make the quantum leap from "judging" others on the basis of their weaknesses to "evaluating" them according to their present and potential strengths

Why ______________________________

How ______________________________

When ______________________________

"Thanks," Doug said, "Wait till I give copies of this to my colleagues!"

I will pay more for the ability
to deal with people than for any other
ability under the sun.

—JOHN D. ROCKEFELLER

7

FROM DRIVING TO LEADING

Everyone was talking about the extraordinary results emanating from Doug's department. Mark Jackson gushed with enthusiasm for Doug, his team and his department's new production records. Every week they were breaking through with new records. One statement remained vivid in Doug's memory: "Doug, congratulations on being a visionary leader with followers that love you and your new leadership style. Can you see now why leadership that leads, works, and why drivers fail?" Doug got the message and nodded. It inspired him to put together a checklist of the traits of a positive motivator—a visionary leader—and the traits of a negative motivator—a driver. With the help of Laura Bosco and other team members, he compiled 20 paradigm-popping shifts or changes. He explained to his team members that a paradigm is an "outstandingly clear or typical example; a model, picture, image, concept or idea."

20 Paradigm-Popping Shifts

Positive Motivators (Visionary Leaders)	Negative Motivators (Drivers)
Asking	Telling
Pulling	Pushing
Looking for strengths	Looking for weaknesses
Generous praise	Grudging compliments
Cooperating with others and self	Competing with others
Value-led	Value-driven
Vision-led	Vision-driven
Open and vulnerable mind	Closed and defensive mind
Expecting the best	Expecting second best or worst
Stressing results	Stressing activity
Crisp and sharp	Sloppy grooming
Empowering others	Diminishing others
Hearing by actively listening	Listening negatively
Loving and caring	Hating and hostile
Learners	Knowers
Goal-oriented	Role-oriented
Welcoming change	Resisting change
Person-centered	Role-centered
"We"	"I"
Crystal-clear integrity	Expedient moral practices

The Power Of "Follow Me"

"Two questions," Doug asked The Mentor. "Are all excellent motivators also excellent leaders? And are all excellent leaders also excellent motivators?"

A broad smile illuminated The Mentor's face. "In a word—yes!" he exuded.

"Good news," Doug later told Laura. "Everyone can learn to be an excellent motivator and visionary leader and then exceed all our expectations!"

"I got it!" Laura beamed.

They agreed that they wanted to get *everyone* involved in this commitment and excitement and these exquisite new results. Doug thought about it and boiled down all he had learned into a powerful motto. He felt he had gained rich insights from The Mentor, and one fact towered above all the others. Doug wished he had known it years ago, and was grateful he knew it now.

It is relatively easy to follow and respond to a real Master Motivator who "walks ahead of the flock" and *pulls.*

And . . .

The greatest statement of motivation ever uttered is, "Follow me." (Whether symbolically, figuratively or literally.)

Therefore . . .

No one can follow or respond to a "motivator" if the motivator is figuratively or literally "behind" the motivatee, *pushing.*

The Mentor had said, "All great motivators, masters of motivation, are motive-led and value-fed.

Doug requested a list of values to feed his mind and spirit as he moved from being a "good Motivator" to becoming like his Mentor, a Master Motivator.

Specific Action Steps

Motives that lead and values that feed include:

- Motivators enjoy life.
- Motivators reach out—they do not retreat inward.
- Motivators cultivate a "lust for learning."
- Motivators expect the best—always.
- Motivators are goal-oriented.
- Motivators help others feel significant.
- Motivators lead by example.
- Motivators provide purpose and direction.
- Motivators are go-givers—not go-getters.
- Motivators respect themselves and others.
- Motivators ask, listen and *hear.*
- Motivators pursue total fitness.
- Motivators radiate warmth and caring.

Leadership is an invisible strand as mysterious as it is powerful. It pulls and it bonds. The most precious and intangible quality of leadership is trust.

—IBM Publications

8

CONTINUOUS ENERGY AND VITALITY

"There is one quality that one seldom ever encounters in books and videos about motivation," The Mentor said, "and yet is extraordinarily important."

Doug was almost startled by the intensity in The Mentor's voice. He knew what followed would be vitally important to his progress.

"What's that?" he asked.

The Mentor replied earnestly, "You've really become a Master Motivator—but here is one more challenge:

"Do you dare to feel just as good as you possibly can?"

Doug found this intriguing. He had always kept himself in good condition. But as "good as possible"? He wanted to know more.

Vital Thoughts and Practices

"You mean just as good as I possibly can? Sure, I'm up to the challenge. What do I need to do?"

The Mentor walked over to his flip chart and wrote as he talked.

A. PHYSICAL FITNESS:

1. A comprehensive physical.
2. A thorough physical workout three or more times each week. Walk as much as possible. Climb stairs when you can rather than using an escalator or elevator.
3. Read a good book on nutrition. Dr. Sheldon Saul Hendler is a leader in the field. There's also *Fit for Life* by Harvey and Marilyn Diamond.

B. MENTAL FITNESS:

1. Establish a regular reading program. Launch or conclude your day with inspired readings. Your public library is a treasure house for this. Visit the self-help and self-improvement section.
2. Regularly review every macro and micro element of the Blueprint for One-on-One Motivation.

C. SPIRITUAL FITNESS:

1. Search and seek to develop, or further strengthen, your own conception of a universal deity. Regular attendance at the church, temple or synagogue of your choice is desirable.
2. Ask a respected member of the clergy to recommend a reading and study program. Get involved!

Keep Reaching!

(Specific Action Steps)

- Vow to become a continuous and perpetual learner. Remember, no one really *follows* a "Knower." *All great motivators keep learning until the day they die!*

- Hold regularly scheduled sessions with your family. Realize that you can learn much that is valuable and real from your children and your spouse. Relish this, and *let them know it!*
- Perhaps the single most powerful characteristic for Master Motivators is that they:

Learn, learn, learn!
Mentor, Mentor, Mentor!
Train, Train, Train!

Do a little more than you're paid to
Give a little more than you have to
Try a little harder than you want to
Aim a little higher than you think possible
And give a lot of thanks to God for
health, family and friends.

—ART LINKLETTER

9

CONTINUOUS FEEDBACK

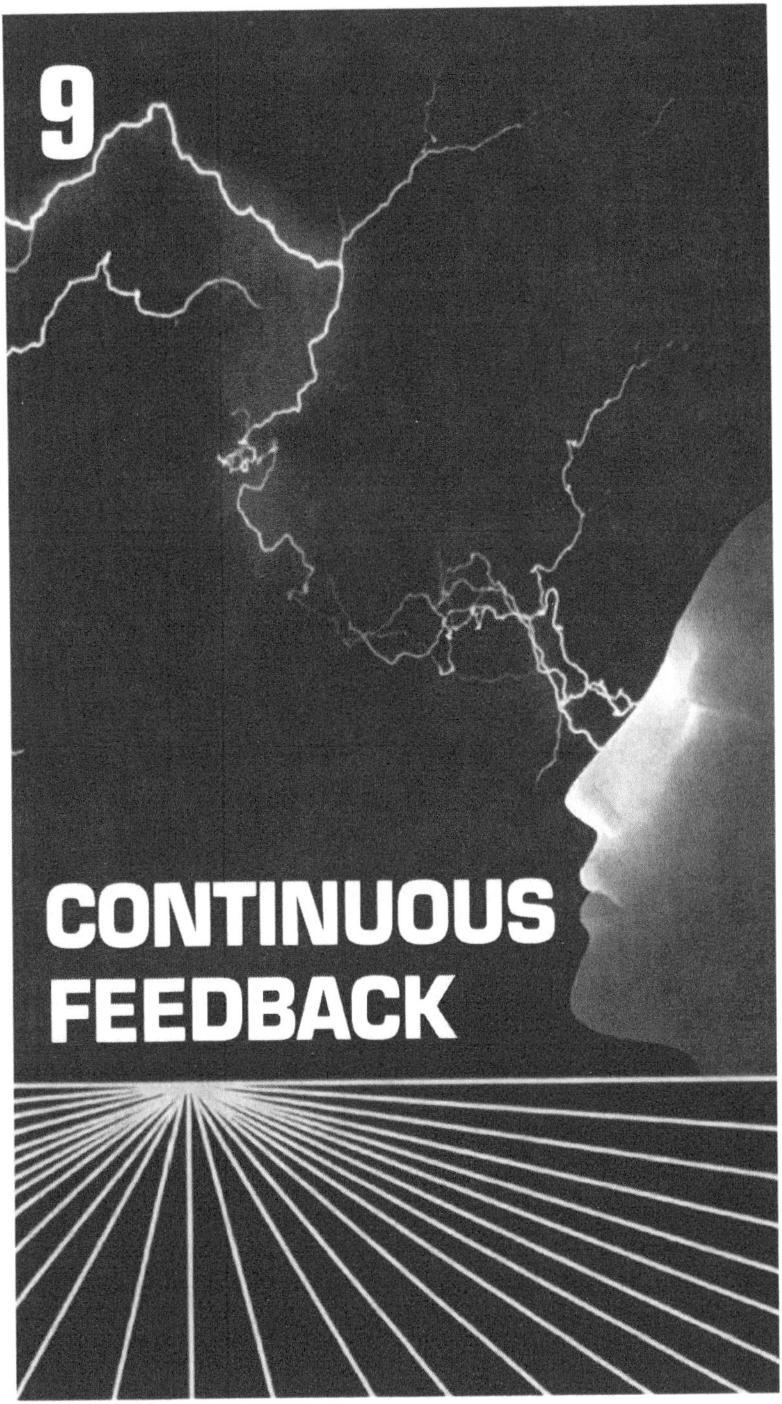

The Five Key Steps in Motivation

The Mentor said, "The central tools of motivation and the tools of feedback are indivisible."

Although he had verified the wisdom of this many times since he first heard it, Doug still remembered how startled and doubting he was at first.

"How can that be?" he had said.

Again, The Mentor smiled and replied, "The tools of all feedback are found in Kipling's 'six honest serving men.' They are:

What
Where
When
Who
How
Why

"The tools of all motivation derive from determining, pursuing and acting on:

What
Where
When
Who
How
Why

Doug mentally reviewed these crucial words. He decided to put them on a 3" x 5" card under his glass desktop and asked his team to do likewise. He leaned back in his chair and pondered the success of his team.

When Laura Bosco walked in a few minutes later, Doug thought of how it was clear to all that Laura would be his successor. Doug was unquestionably on his way onward, upward, and Godward—as all Master Motivators are.

"Okay," Laura said, grinning, "you promised to tell me the *five key steps.* I've certainly learned a lot from you and have studied the eight phases in the Blueprint for One-on-One Motivation. But what is the boiled-down, distilled essence of motivation?"

"I'm all ready for you," Doug said warmly as he flipped back the cover sheet on his flip chart. He had been working on five essential elements of motivation, a way to break down all he had learned to kernels of knowledge.

"Here they are!"

This is what Laura saw:

Master Motivation at a Glance

1. CLEAR EXPECTATIONS (goals and motives) requested firmly with caring confidence and consistency.
2. BASE ALL REQUESTS (not orders) on known and suspected strengths and on the empathic awareness of needs, desires and fears.
3. INSURE that full training, mentoring and support are scheduled at all times.
4. CONTINUOUS, CONFIDENT AND CARING FEEDBACK. When firmness is needed, *mean what you say!*
5. EXPECT THE BEST, being firm and caring. Provide generous earned praise, and an example of constant commitment to *learning.*

"Any questions?" Doug asked.

"I'm sure I'll have some after I've digested this," said Laura, "and I'll really look forward to continuing these sessions, especially as you move on up the ladder." Doug smiled pensively as he remembered yet another morsel of wisdom from The Mentor.

Motivating and leading people to become all they can be is one of the greatest thrills that exists.

The world belongs to the energetic.

—Ralph Waldo Emerson

10

THE MASTER MOTIVATOR LOOKS AHEAD

The Monday after the award ceremony, Doug reflected on how great he felt knowing he had received the first Master Motivator award from the Profitable Products Company. He had come a long way, but he couldn't stop now and rest on his laurels. The future beckoned and he was ready to meet it.

The 18 months of tutelage by The Mentor had produced changes that would last the rest of his life.

- His family life and parenting skills had become better than his aspirations, and more exciting than his hopes.
- Marya, Dan and Sandi appeared to be thriving on the new goal-oriented direction of the family. Love abounded with their new warmth and sharing.
- His circle of friends in the community and in the company had become pleasingly extensive and expansive.
- His promotion was going to provide challenge, growth opportunities and mind-toughening expectations in abundance.
- There would be mountains to climb and rivers to cross, but he knew he'd be ready.

Sensing a presence in the doorway, Doug looked up. It was The Mentor. Face shining, The Mentor said, "Doug, you are an extraordinary student. I'm proud of your progress. I've loved working with you and I just want you to know that I'd love to continue our friendship and relationship."

Doug Sanchez stood, smiling broadly. Tears flooded his eyes as he reached to shake The Mentor's hand and said, "Isn't life great?"

The world is moved by
highly-motivated people, by enthusiasts,
by men and women who want
something very much and
believe very much.

—JOE BATTEN

1. *Think and Grow Rich,* by Dr. Napoleon Hill (New York: Fawcett Crest Publishing, 1937). This book is an in-depth study of the 500 most influential and effective business people, leaders, thinkers and politicians of Hill's time. He distilled 13 principles all used to achieve greatness. These principles work for everyone who works them. Employ them, starting now, to benefit you, your family, your company and your work.

2. *Chicken Soup for the Soul,* by Mark Victor Hansen and Jack Canfield (Deerfield Beach, Fla.: Health Communications, Inc., 1993). Master Motivators are all master storytellers and communicators. Read this masterful book of 101 true stories. Memorize several, and use them one-on-one and before groups. Notice how well you can enchant your listeners and how a well-chosen, well-told story can illustrate your point.

3. *Tough-Minded Leadership,* by Joe Batten (New York: AMACOM, 1989). Real leaders are tough-minded yet tender-hearted result-getters. Joe is the pioneering thinker who billionaire Ross Perot credits with getting him to think bigger and more effectively.

4. *The Richest Man in Babylon,* by George Classon (New York: Bantam, 1985). All motivators need to manage their resources. Classon's parable teaches readers how to become debt-free, stress-free and financially free.

5. *The Power of Positive Thinking,* by Dr. Norman Vincent Peale (Greenwich, Conn.: Fawcett Crest Publishing, 1952). This classic will speak to your soul. More than 25 million copies have been sold.

6. *Fit or Fat,* by Covert Bailey (Boston: Houghton Mifflin Co., 1984). Motivators with high energy motivate better than motivators with low energy. Covert motivates you to get and stay forever fit.

7. *The One-Minute Bible* (available from Mark's office—call 800-433-2314 or 714-759-9304). Everyone says they want to read the Bible and never do. Now you can read one page, one minute per day and finish the Bible cover-to-cover in 366 days. You'll be wowed to know what the greatest motivators in the history of the world did and why.

8. *Building A Total Quality Culture*, by Joe Batten (Menlo Park, Calif.: Crisp Publications, Inc., 1992). How to systematically create an organizational culture that optimizes the motivational potential of everyone.
9. *The Greatest Salesman in the World*, by Og Mandino (New York: Bantam, 1983). Og's classic bestseller inspires readers to sell themselves on living up to their full potential and manifesting their inner greatness. Over 15 million copies sold.
10. *The Five Major Pieces to the Life Puzzle*, by Jim Rohn and Ron Reynolds (Irving, Tex.: Jim Rohn International, 1991). Jim takes an in-depth look into the reasons certain people succeed and others don't. He covers the key components to success—philosophy, attitude, activity, results and lifestyle.
11. *The Treasury of Quotes*, by Jim Rohn (Irving, Tex.: Jim Rohn International, 1995). Over 365 inspirational quotes on more than 60 topics.
12. *Make It a Winning Life*, by Wolf J. Rinke, Ph.D. (Rockville, Maryland: Achievement Publishers, 1992). Dr. Wolf J. Rinke teaches you six easy-to-learn principles that will transform your life and help you succeed in life, love and business more effectively than ever before.

1. *To Sir With Love,* featuring Sidney Poitier. Every motivator is challenged to gain the respect, admiration and attention of his or her team or class. "Sir" is a great and inspiring teacher in the inner city who converts uninspired students into great ones.

2. *Stand and Deliver,* starring Edward James Olmos. Jaime Escalante takes unruly, cut-up barrio kids and inspires them to study and learn calculus. The students score in the top 4 percentile of the S.A.T. and win scholarships to Harvard, Wharton and Yale.

3. *Conrack,* featuring John Voigt as a teacher in rural Mississippi. He reframes the students' education, lives and futures, inspiring them to look beyond their limited world..

4. *My Fair Lady,* which is from the book *Pygmalion.* George Bernard Shaw teaches the Pygmalion effect, which is self-fulfilling prophecy. Greatness seen and announced in another manifests. (Note: This is slightly chauvinistic due to the period in which it was produced. Forgive this, and see what's possible when a great and inspiring teacher pulls the greatness out of one of his pupils.)

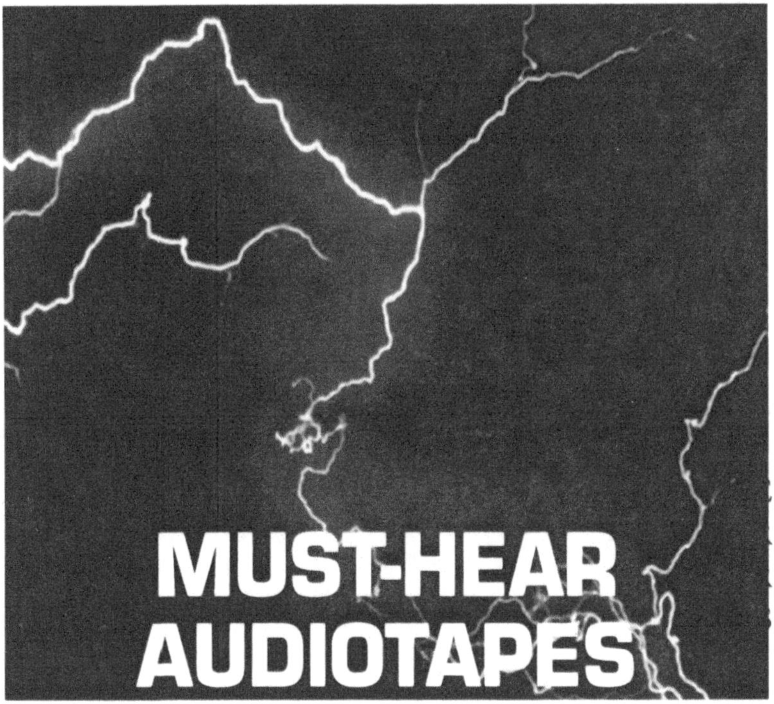

1. *World's Greatest Goal-Setter, by John Goddard.*
2. *Self-Esteem and Peak Performance,* by Jack Canfield.
3. *Dare to Win,* by Mark Victor Hansen.
4. *The Greatest Secret,* by Joe Batten.
5. *Secrets of Tough-Minded Winners,* by Joe Batten.
6. *Chicken Soup for the Soul,* by Jack Canfield and Mark Victor Hansen.

7. *Visualizing Is Realizing,* by Mark Victor Hansen.
8. *The Challenge to Succeed in the 90's,* by Jim Rohn.
9. *The Art of Exceptional Living,* by Jim Rohn.

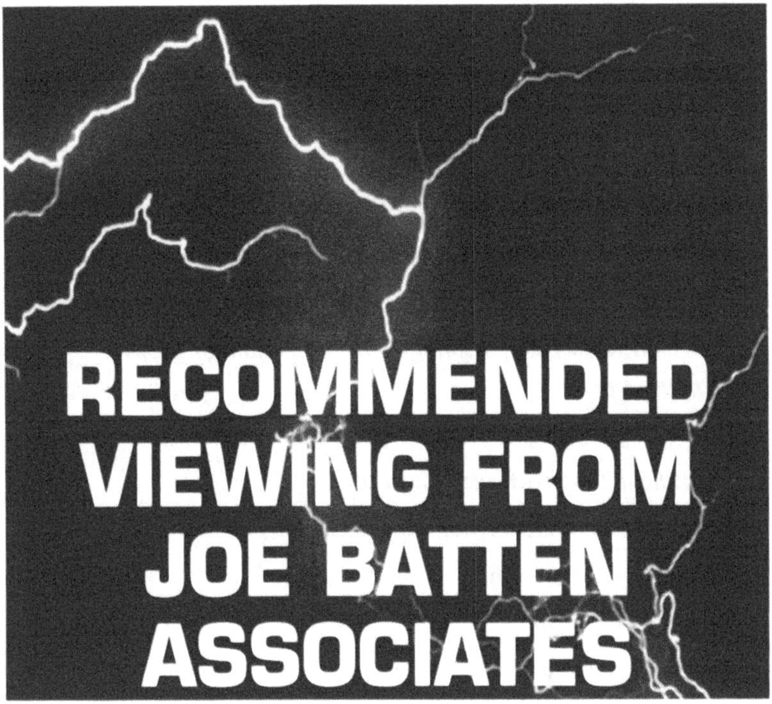

Joe Batten Videos

Tough-Minded Leadership

Keep Reaching

When Commitments Aren't Met

Solving Employee Conflict

Power-Packed Selling: The Trust Factor in Customer Relationships

The Face-to-Face Payoff: Dynamics of the Interview

The Nuts & Bolts of Performance Appraisal

I Understand—You Understand: The Dynamics of Transactional Analysis

The ABCs of Decision Making

A Recipe for Results: Making Management by Objective Work

No-Nonsense Delegation

The Nuts & Bolts of Health Care Management Communication

Tough-Minded Interpersonal Communication for Law Enforcement

Evaluating the Performance of Law Enforcement Personnel

Creating a Tough-Minded Culture

Tough-Minded Supervision for Law Enforcement

Commitment Pays Off

Friendly Persuasion

Keep on Reaching

Trust Your Team

Dare to Dream

Revitalize with Exercise

Joe Batten Films/Videos

Ask for the Order and Get It (Chicago: Dartnell)

Your Price Is Right, Sell It (Dartnell)

Manage Your Time to Build Your Territory (Dartnell)

When You've Turned Down . . . Turn On (Dartnell)

Your Sales Presentation . . . Make It a Winner (Dartnell)

Management by Example (Rockville, Md.: BNA)

The Man in the Mirror (BNA)

RECOMMENDED VIEWING FROM JOE BATTEN ASSOCIATES

The Fully Functioning Individual (BNA)

The Fully Functioning Organization (BNA)

The Fully Functioning Society (BNA)

(To order call 800-234-3176.)

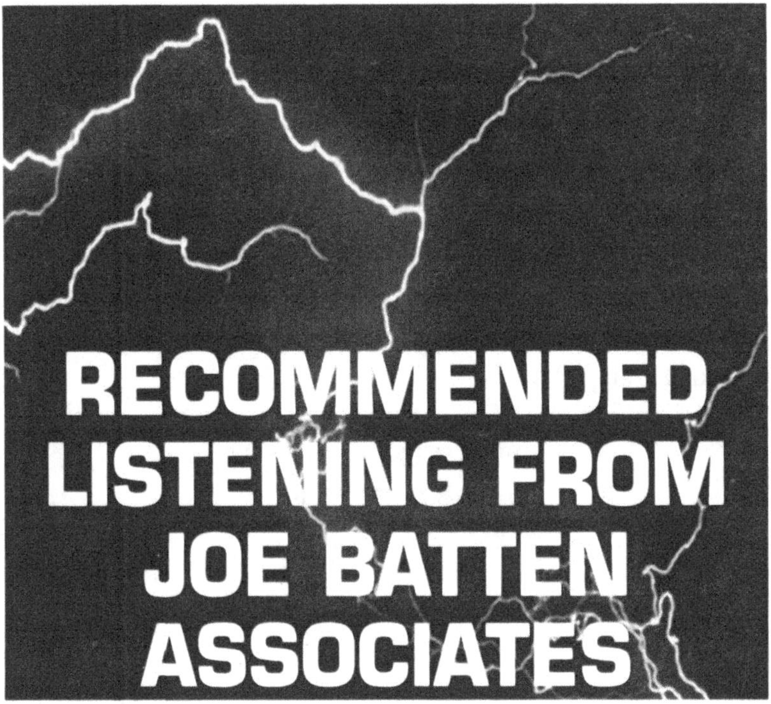

Audiocassettes

How to Apply the Tough-Minded Decision-Making Process

The Nuts & Bolts of Health Care Management Communication

Tough-Minded Supervision for Law Enforcement

How to Install a Tough-Minded Performance Appraisal System

Joe Batten on Management

The Greatest Secret

Face-to-Face Motivation

Face-to-Face Management

Secrets of Tough-Minded Winners

How to Exceed Yourself

(To order call 800-247-5087.)

If you would like to receive additional assessment materials or other information concerning workshops, seminars, consulting or speaking, call:

JOE BATTEN ASSOCIATES
1-800-234-3176

Autry, James A. *Love and Profit.* New York: Morrow, 1991.

Batten, Joe. *Building a Total Quality Culture.* Menlo Park, Calif.: Crisp Publications, 1992.

____________. *Beyond Management by Objectives,* New York: AMACOM, 1966.

____________. *Developing a Tough-Minded Climate for Results.* New York: American Management Association, 1965.

____________. *Tough-Minded Leadership.* New York: AMACOM, 1989.

____________. *Tough-Minded Management,* 3rd ed. New York: American Management Association, 1978.

____________. *Tough-Minded Parenting.* Nashville: Broadman Press, 1991.

Bennis, Warren and Burt Nanus. *Leaders.* New York: Harper & Row, 1985.

Burns, James M. *Leadership.* New York: Harper & Row, 1985.

Canfield, Jack and Mark Victor Hansen. *Chicken Soup For the Soul.* Deerfield Beach, Fla.: Health Communications, Inc., 1993.

Cohen, William C. *The Art of the Leader.* New York: Prentice-Hall, 1990.

Cox, Allen. *The Making of the Achiever.* New York: Rodd, Mead and Company, 1984.

Crosby, Philip B. *Quality Without Tears.* New York: McGraw-Hill, 1984.

Deal, Terence E. and Allan A. Kennedy. *Corporate Culture.* Reading, Mass.: Addison-Wesley, 1982.

DePree, Max. *Leadership Is an Art.* New York: Doubleday, 1990.

Garfield, Charles. *Peak Performers.* New York: Morrow, 1986.

Gerber, Michael. *The E-Myth.* New York: Harper Business, 1986.

Goble, Frank. *Excellence in Leadership.* New York: AMACOM, 1972.

Hansen, Mark Victor. *Dare to Win.* Newport Beach, Calif.: Mark Victor Hansen, 1988.

Hill, Napoleon. *Think and Grow Rich.* New York: Fawcett Crest Publishing, 1937.

Kanter, Rosabeth Moss. *When Giants Learn to Dance.* New York: Simon & Schuster, 1990.

Kouzes, James M. and Barry Z. Posner. *The Leadership Challenge.* San Francisco: Jossey-Gass, 1987.

Manz, Charles C. and Henry P. Sims. *Super Leadership.* New York: Prentice-Hall, 1989.

Miller, Lawrence M. *American Spirit: Visions of a New Corporate Culture.* New York: Morrow, 1984.

Morton, Michael S. Scott. *The Corporation of the 1990s.* New York: Oxford University Press, 1991.

Nanus, Bert. *The Leader's Edge.* Chicago: Contemporary Books, 1990.

Pilzer, Paul Zane. *Unlimited Wealth.* New York: Crown, 1990.

Rohn, Jim and Ronald L. Reynolds. *The Five Major Pieces to the Life Puzzle.* Irving, Tex.: Jim Rohn International, 1991.

____________. *The Seasons of Life.* Irving, Tex.: Jim Rohn International, 1981.

Schein, Edgar H. *Organizational Culture and Leadership.* San Francisco: Jossey-Bass, 1985.

Senge, Peter. *The Fifth Discipline.* New York: Doubleday, 1990.

Tucker, Robert B. *Managing the Future.* New York: G.P. Putnam and Sons, 1991.

Van Ekeran, Glenn. *The Speaker's Source Book.* New York: Prentice-Hall, 1988.

Waterman, Robert H. Jr. *The Renewal Factor.* New York: Bantam Books, 1987.

West, Ross. *How to Be Happier in the Job You Sometimes Can't Stand.* Nashville: Broadman Press, 1991.

Youngs, Bettie B. *Getting Back Together: Creating a New Relationship with Your Partner and Making It Last.* New York: Bob Adams, Inc., 1991.

____________. *How to Develop Self-Esteem in Your Child: 6 Vital Ingredients.* New York: Ballantine, 1992.

____________. *Safeguarding Your Teenager from the Dragons of Life: A Guide to the Adolescent Years.* Deerfield Beach, Fla.: Health Communications, Inc., 1993.

____________. *Values from the Heartland.* Deerfield Beach, Fla.: Health Communications, Inc., 1995.

Ziglar, Zig. *Top Performance.* New York: Berkley Books, 1990.

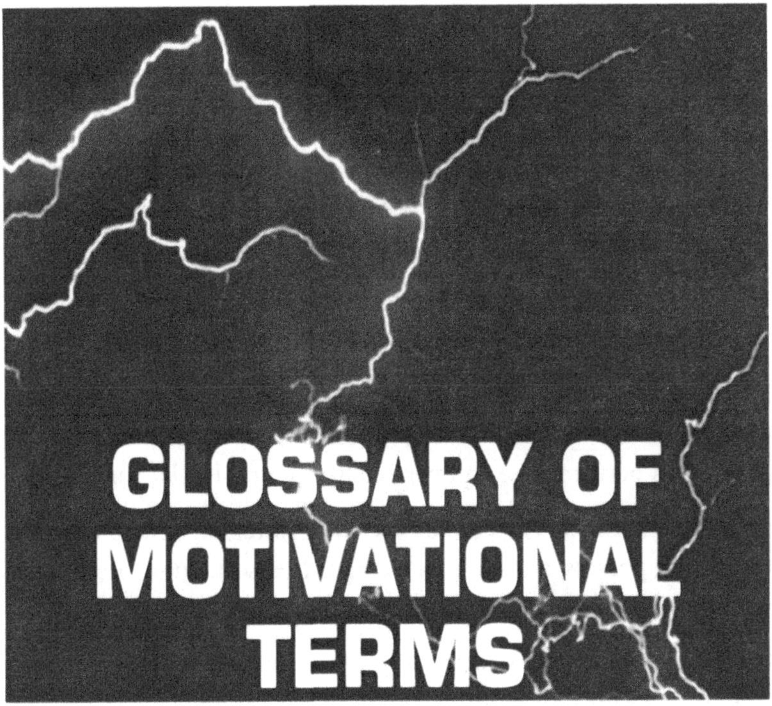

Accountability. The "ability to account" for the extent to which a commitment is met.

Action Plan. A sequenced and prioritized chronology of intent, commitment and tactics. Includes defining what one is going to accomplish and some of the key activities involved in achieving that goal.

Activity. Motion toward a clearly targeted result. Activity is something one does, as contrasted with something one gets done (result).

Aggressiveness. Initiative that is primarily self-serving. Not to be confused with assertiveness, which uses one's strengths for purpose of building.

Amateur or Obsolete Competitor. One who competes with others rather than with one's own self-generated goals. One who seeks to beat or defeat another person or group.

Analyze. To divide the whole into its component parts (who, what, where, when, how, why) in order to determine the nature and function of, and proportion and relationship between, the parts.

Appraisal. Determination of the value and possibilities implicit in a person's performance and personality at a particular time.

Assertiveness. The vulnerable exposure of strengths. Since strengths are all we possess, and thus all we have to assert, vulnerability permits the full use of these strengths without defensiveness.

Build. The blending of strengths into a composite whole. Key elements in tough-minded team-building are those in which the team is armed with a positive philosophy, guided with principles, guided by practices and sustained by faith.

Builder. The CEO who stands tall is, above all, a builder. Committed to vision, stretch, empowerment, synergy, responsiveness, flexibility and, importantly, toughness of mind. A builder ensures that all dimensions of each P in the pyramid (*see* P Pyramid) are intensely focused on creation, growth and building.

Candor. Applied truth. In the tough-minded lexicon, this involves openness, vulnerability, awareness of the needs of others and a genuine desire to build them.

Caring. Consistent manifestation of concern for and affirmation of others. The perception that all people are right until proved wrong and that each person is a bundle of strengths and possibilities.

Climate. The temperature of the human environment in which one finds oneself; the "feel" or the "chemistry," often more sensed than known.

Climate for Mistakes. An environment that calls for and reinforces constant experimentation, creativity, innovation and change. Encourages the practice of "failing forward." Mistakes within reason are rewarded rather than penalized.

Coach. A person who helps others develop insights and actions to achieve mutually understood goals. This pertains particularly to helping others identify, surface, fuse and focus their present and potential strengths.

Collaborate. Coordination in action. A blend of strengths to produce positive symbiosis and synergy.

Commitment. An internalized, then externalized, concentration of desire and energy focused on various degrees of achievement. An "integrity of intent."

Communication. Shared meaning, shared understanding.

Compensation. Full value, psychological or financial, provided or received for energy expended in accomplishing results.

Confront. To address openly, honestly and vulnerably that which needs to be challenged. The reverse of expedience, obliqueness, deviousness or avoidance.

Consistency. Unity of thought, word or deed over a continuum of time, space or relationship.

Consultive Decision-Making. A decision-making process in which the leader involves team members and secures their best input prior to making any major decisions. The tough-minded leader places a premium in asking, listening and hearing. Thus, when he or she makes a decision and stresses the logical deployment of strengths, team members are expected to meet lean, stretching commitments. Clear-cut accountability is a crucial operational requirement here.

Control. An end result of interactive processes involving clarity of expectation and the achievement thereof. Control is not a tool per se. It is a result of excellence in applying the other concepts in the tough-minded leadership system.

Conviction. Individual and team evidence of strong persuasion; the manner in which strong commitment, fueled by involvement, is practiced; fulfillment of a pledge.

Coordination. Shared meaning and shared understanding that permits and requires the synchronized effort of appropriate people to achieve mutually understood goals.

Counsel. *See* Coach. They are indivisible.

Criticize. To evaluate the results of analyses and identify the values or strengths therein. To build on those strengths by seeking to improve the situation, person or thing.

Culture. The pervasive philosophy, central values, beliefs, attitudes and practices of an organization, and the micro elements that make things happen.

Customer-Led Automated Marketing System (CLAMS). A total operational system fed by imaginatively programmed touch-screened computers to provide constant and comprehensive customer input as a basis for ongoing evaluation and improvement of the entire P Pyramid.

Cybernetic. (From the Greek word, *kybernetes*, meaning helmsman.) A self-correcting system whose function is perpetuated by a closed-loop or serve mechanism.

Develop. To generate, synthesize, nurture and ultimately create something better.

Dignity. The worth, significance and uniqueness of a person; an awareness of intrinsic worth. Clear, consistent expectations and a constant search for and focus on strengths affirm this dignity.

Directive. Words or actions, felt or implied, that arbitrarily indicate an action or result desired. Tends to suggest "compression and pushing" rather than "evoking and stretching" (as in Expective).

Discipline. Training and development that builds, molds and strengthens; lean, clean, focused behavior.

Dissatisfaction. A preoccupation with past failures; a tendency to dwell on what didn't work. This term should not be confused with unsatisfaction, which is a healthy, hungry desire to change, grow and move onward and upward.

Doubt Your Doubts. To consistently and responsively subject one's doubts to positive analysis and evaluation to determine latent possibilities.

Dream. A deeply felt hope of the possible. Dreams lift and move individuals and organizations to the highest level.

Emotional Conflict. A blend of emotions needed to ensure that knowledge or information is transmuted and transmitted into learning. A gestalt of feelings.

Emotional Context. A blend of various emotions such as anger, fear, disgust, grief, joy and surprise used to achieve learning or modification of behavior. A bland relationship between two people in a business environment seldom results in much real learning.

Empathy. The imaginative projection of one's consciousness into the consciousness of another. The ability to put oneself in another person's shoes.

Empower. To create and foster a relationship in which the other person or persons understand their significance, possibilities and strengths. People who are empowered have a clear understanding of their authority, responsibility, accountability and valued role on the team, and they have autonomy that is symbiotic with others. You obtain power by giving power.

Evaluate. To identify the relative value of a person, place, thing or relationship. The values (strengths) are often revealed by analysis.

Excellence. What happens when you give an undertaking your best shot and know it.

Exemplars. Leaders whose personas and actions represent the essence of what they say and expect.

Expectation. A desire, want or need communicated in the form of a clear request. The ultimate gift, it says to others, "I value and appreciate your possibilities."

Expective. A more specific statement of expectation; a clear oral or written request. As contrasted with a directive, it is designed to stretch rather than to compress, to pull rather than to push.

Faith. Belief in and commitment to causes, quests and affirmations that transcend self-concern.

Feedback. Information that clearly indicates the progress and corrective needs of the ongoing project or undertaking.

Flexibility and Resilience. The opposite of rigidity. The living and committed responsiveness to possibilities, difficulties and opportunities.

Focus. A point at which energy converges; concentrated centering of effort. A focused team shares these perceptions and acts accordingly.

Forgiveness. A requisite for growth, happiness and exponential renewal. As we develop a lifestyle that is based on being for-giving rather than being for-getting, we become capable of forgiving.

Free Enterprise. Freedom of individual action to chart and accomplish a full measure of individual achievement—economically, politically, socially and spiritually. Includes the freedom to develop the whole and apply full talents to stretching work assignments.

Fully Functioning Team. The reverse of a dysfunctional team. A team that epitomizes and validates the tough-minded principles in action. A group that consistently meets, surpasses and develops new dimensions of goal actualization.

Gestalt. A structure in which the response of a person or an organism to a situation is a complete whole rather than simply the sum of the parts or elements; a total configuration of factors.

G Forces. The figurative pull of gravity. Negative G forces of the past are passive, self-defeating attitudes and practices that retard and even reverse growth and forward movement. Positive G forces of the future are passionate attitudes and practices that help pull and guide the leader to move toward the future in the most productive, energetic and positively magnetic way. Like a compass, positive G forces guide and pull.

Goal. Something one wishes to accomplish. Broader and more timeless than an objective. Expressed as a desired and targeted happening.

Go-Giver. A positive term replacing the cliché "go-getter." A go-giver is a tough-minded person who knows that one can achieve much more when major energies are directed toward giving encouragement, knowledge, inspiration and understanding to others rather than seeking self-aggrandizement only.

Grace. A special warmth felt and expressed toward all other human beings. The nature of grace is an absence of pettiness and self-concern. A living manifestation of the belief that a person should devote major energies to doing something *for* others and not *to* others.

Gratitude. Thoughts, feelings and actions that reflect and transmit appreciation and earned praise.

Hard. Rigid, compressed, repressed, depressed, oppressed, brittle, dead, weak. The reverse of toughness.

Incident File. A document in which key episodes (both positive and negative) are recorded. To be used for development coaching and counseling.

Individual. In the tough-minded vocabulary, this term means the opposite of a rebel. Rebels live, talk and work in terms of what they are against; individuals live, talk and work in terms of what they are for.

Innovation. Newness in action. Ever-searching, ever-changing concepts, methods, research and application.

Integrity. Strength, reality, authenticity, toughness.

Interdependent. Reciprocal interaction of mutually dependent team members. Such interaction becomes synergistic when the individual team members are provided (equipped) with feelings of significance, constant learning, positive values and examples, focus, and clear expectations.

Intuitive Leadership. The demonstrated capacity to take correct actions without necessarily knowing why. Accurate guesses, whether educated or merely sensed. A feel, a sense, a sensation in the gut of what is appropriate. Quick and ready insight.

Involvement. Joint and shared use of talents to develop, clarify and achieve symbiotic relationships and synergistic results.

Job Description. A listing of key result requirements that constitute or define a job or position.

Judge. To form subjective conclusions about another. Judgments project our negative feelings about ourselves into others; they are a projection of weaknesses. This is the reverse of evaluate.

Key Result Areas. Major areas of an individual position or job. They are usually determined so that objectives or standards will be established for all significant responsibilities of the position. Term may also be used to apply to a major emphasis of an enterprise or project.

Kinesics or Body English. The study of body movements, facial expressions and so on as ways of communicating.

Lead. To be in front, figuratively. To lift, guide, expect, empower, communicate and achieve synergistic results.

Leadership. The exercise of a system of expectations—an ever-changing, ever-dynamic gestalt of interacting minds—designed to mobilize and maximize the most effective use of strengths to achieve objectives.

Leadership by Expectation. Leadership in which a complete and pervasive system of expectations is established throughout the organization and is fueled by the logical deployment of strengths. Leadership by expectation involves the belief that people are the alpha and omega of all organizational success. Such a leader practices virtually all the principles and methods in this book.

Leadership by Renewal. The consistent practice of the principles and methods in this book with primacy given to the belief that all team members are more productive and actualized when they are reaching, growing, involved, empowered and discovering new feelings of individual significance. It is a tough-minded axiom that a leader must first become this kind of person in order to provide true leadership by renewal.

Love. A feeling of brotherhood and good will toward other people. Tough-minded leaders express love via disciplined commitment to build rather than to destroy, to enhance rather than to diminish all associates and team members, through every thought, word and action. Although it is an ideal, tough-minded leaders seek to build this emphasis on enhancement pervasively throughout the organization's P Pyramid.

Loyalty. A quality or action of steadfastly adhering to one's beliefs in a person or thing by every thought, word or action.

Management by Objectives. A management style where, ostensibly, all decisions and actions are executed for the purpose of achieving and exceeding clearly defined and agreed-upon objectives.

Management Process. In the tough-minded management lexicon, this means the following sequence: research, vision or mission, plan, organize, coordinate, execute, control.

Mission. A stretching, guiding and reinforcing statement of intent and commitment.

Motivation. Motive-action; action to achieve motive. Motive (results, objectives, goals) is developed and then action plans are designed to accomplish it.

Motive Power. Focused and positive use of energy to achieve a motive or motives. One's personal motor that enables one to reach and fulfill a motive.

Negative. Any action that involves retreating from the challenge and discipline required to achieve positive results.

Nice Guy. One who is affected, self-deprecating, insincere, overly subtle; hence, evasive and untrustworthy. Used in this context to mean a person who chooses the easier alternative and rationalizes this action with "nice" clichés. One who retreats from the requirements of demanding self-discipline.

Nurture. To provide insights, expectations, reinforcement; asking, listening and hearing that help people grow.

Objective. Something one wants to achieve. A specific statement of quality, quantity and time values.

Open Listening. Truly open "hearing" with heart, mind and soul. A felt and expressed desire to truly understand another person.

Organization. "Organ in action." In business, government and other kinds of endeavors, the collective functioning of a group to achieve mission, goals and objectives.

Organize. To blend resources logistically to achieve objectives; to deploy strengths logically.

Passion. Intense, focused feelings fed in synchromeshed conjunction by the value system described in this book.

Passive. Yielding, quiescent, nonresponsive, with a low level of reaction. The "bland leading the bland."

Performance. Discernible and productive actions moving beyond target or intent and actually fulfilling commitment.

Performance Standards. A baseline level of achievement. Commonly defined in the literature as, "A standard indicates performance is satisfactory when . . ." Meeting standard performance is the basic requirement for maintaining a position. Extra rewards should be bestowed only when the standard is exceeded.

Philosophy. A body of truths and firm beliefs. Organizationally it is the basis for the development of mission, goals, objectives, organization, expective action plans and controls.

Plan. An orderly assortment of actions designed to fulfill a mission or accomplish a goal or objective. An objective by itself is not a plan; it is only the basis for one.

Positive Stress. The opposite of negative stress, which causes dissonant disaster and distress; positive stress is healthy, intensely focused energy applied to positive goals.

Possibility Team. A dynamic group of people assembled to blend strengths to discover, recommend and achieve innovative improvement in all dimensions of the organization.

Power. Qualities emanating from the leader that exert compass-like pull, both subtle and overt. Such qualities provide both direction and attraction, purpose and pull. Positive, forward-focused influence.

Power Teams. A team that is lifted and stretched toward new and exciting levels of positive achievement. A team that is value-centered and value-led.

P Pyramid. The pyramidal triangle that presents the following sequence of Ps: Philosophy (principles), Policies (programs), Processes (practices), Programs (people), Purpose (profit). These Ps represent the complete infrastructure of any organization.

Presence. A total appearance or impression projected by an individual. A person with presence emanates confidence and effectiveness and inspires the confidence of others.

Purpose. An overriding, lifting, stretching end to be attained.

Quality. The degree of excellence a person or object possesses. *Also see* Total Quality.

Rebel. A person who knows, and is primarily motivated by, what he or she is against; to know what one is against and be motivated accordingly. *See also* Individual.

Renewal. Innovation and renovation. The process of making fresh, strong and good; new physical, mental and spiritual strength.

Renewal Organization. The type of organization in which all the Ps, with emphasis on the people, are geared toward the practice of the contents of this book.

Respect. Feelings, felt and expressed, that reflect enhanced awareness of the dignity, worth and individuality of another person.

Responsibility. Response-ability, or ability to respond. Responding fully to the pledge of a commitment; responding in a manner consistent with full integrity.

Results. The final happening. Not to be confused with a measurement of a result.

Rigid Thermometer. A descriptive term for a person whose attitudes and actions simply register the temperature of the climate in which he or she functions.

Self-Actualized. Focused, activated and fueled by the entire value system in this book with particular emphasis on clarity of expectations, building on strengths and enhancement and empowerment of the team. The self-actualized leader lives and works within the context of a transcendent vision of the possible.

Self-Confidence. An individual's belief that he or she is significant and good. A growing awareness of one's own strengths and, often, a heightened zest for strong, testing and confrontive challenges.

Self-Discipline. A commitment of self—in discipleship—to worthwhile courses of action, programs of development and fitness. Most effective when focused on goals that transcend personal gain.

Self-Esteem. (*See* Self-Confidence.) Esteem is, perhaps, a more immediate and now sense of confidence.

Self-Led Teams. Where focus, commitment and follow-through are generated from within the team. The synergistic conjunction of motivated individual members of the team.

Service. The ongoing product of a passionate commitment to fulfill the wants, needs and possibilities of others.

Servo-System. A closed-loop cybernetic process that provides for macro-organizational feedback and responsiveness as well as micro-organizational feedback and responsiveness. Such macro and micro servo-systems will make possible the kind of responsiveness to customers that must shape the volatile leadership wave of tomorrow.

Significance. The feeling that a person "counts," is real and is achieving good, stretching and relevant accomplishments in life.

Social Gestalt. A dynamic interweaving of individual behavior patterns that produces group accomplishment greater than the sum of its parts.

Sophisticated. Artificial, highly complicated, refined; maintaining a facade that obscures the basic truths of a situation.

Strategy. A careful plan or method focused on macro goals. Completed, fulfilled and sometimes exceeded with the aid of tough-minded tactics and micro-focused action steps.

Strengths. The true realities in life. Conversely, weaknesses are only what is absent or lacking. Strengths are the only building blocks, the only resources one can employ in every dimension of life. The meaning of strength and integrity is the same.

Strengths Bank. A computerized data base containing the salient strengths of all relevant personnel. The bank is accessed regularly to truly practice the logical deployment of strengths. All major assignments are made and decisions are conditioned by such deployment. Since strengths are indeed the only reality in a person, the Strengths Bank enables an organization to move forward on the basis of total reality. Weaknesses are regarded merely as missing strengths or insufficiently developed strengths.

Stress. *See* Positive Stress.

Stretch. A questing, reaching, search for a better way.

Symbiosis. A relationship where living or working together provides and enhances mutual advantage.

Synergy. Since all that goes up must ultimately converge, synergy is the magnified impact of a confluence or synthesis of strengths. In shorthand, 2 + 2 = 5 or more. The whole is greater than the sum of the parts.

Synthesize. To combine the values and strengths of individuals discovered during an evaluation.

System. Dynamic reciprocating aggregate of sequenced actions to achieve properly determined objectives.

System of Values. A complete and functionally compatible combination of essential truths. Values are the subjective interpretation of the immutable laws of the universe that shape and guide human reactions. The orderly expression and transfer of tough-minded values into practices is the essential process involved in building a climate of productivity.

Team. A combination of people or other productive units working in dynamic and positive conjunction with each other to produce synergistic results. A group that shares a common toughness of mind.

Team Development. To elicit and evolve possibilities for internally generated growth. To identify, unify and synergize individual strengths. Thus, a whole greater than the sum of its parts.

Teaming. An ongoing process; a leading-edge example of all of the "We" factors in action. (*See* "We" Feeling.)

Team Motivation. Motive power in action, expressed synergistically. A tough-minded blend of pull (goals) and push (accountability).

Team Synergy. Sacred meaning, values, beliefs, strengths, commitment, stretch and reward.

Tenacity. Resilience, staying power, ability to bounce back. Determination to prevail through thick and thin. Focused endurance.

Theory X. A management style described by Douglas McGregor in *The Human Side of Enterprise.* It illustrates the reverse of all that is advocated in this book by stressing the use of organizational rank and directiveness as one's first expedient.

Theory Y. Another management style created by Douglas McGregor. It places a premium on caring about people and empowering them to give their best efforts to team accomplishment. It is in general agreement with tough-minded leaders.

Theory Z. A management style described in William Ouchi's book *Theory Z,* it is based on 13 steps practiced by leading Japanese companies. This approach derives from numerous applications of tough-minded management techniques initially introduced to Japanese business people by Konosuke Matsushita, then chairman of the board of Matsushita Industries. He has credited Batten, Batten, Hudson & Swab, Inc. as the source of these seminal techniques.

Tomorrow-Mindedness. An approach in which all the Ps in the organization are designed and instrumented to anticipate, create and innovate to meet requirements of the future. A tomorrow-minded leader is responsive rather than reactive.

Tool. A useable resource or combination of resources to instrument a desirable level of achievement. Something one usually employs directly to get something done.

Total Quality. Integrity of function and composition, from alpha to omega.

Total Quality Culture. Concentrating all people and resources on a never-ending quest for greater quality in every dimension of the culture of the organization. Beyond Total Quality Management (TQM), TQC is pervasive.

Tough. The integrity of a substance, person, place, thing or feeling. Characterized by tenacity, resilience, flexibility, durability and suppleness.

Tough Mind and Tender Heart. A synergistic blend of attitudes and actions that reflect stretch, tenacity, discipline, warmth and caring.

Tough-Minded. Open, resilient, growing, changing, questing, stretching quality of mind. Having an infinite capacity for growth and change. *See* Tough and Tough-Minded Leader.

Tough-Minded Competitor. One who consistently confronts his or her possibilities, competes with his or her own self-generated goals, and constantly seeks to become all he or she can be.

Tough-Minded Leader. The kind of leader who, much like a compass, provides direction and magnetic pull. The TML "walks in front of the flock" and exemplifies the system of values and practices that this book is all about.

Tough-Minded Thermostat. A descriptive term for a person whose attitudes, commitment and actions change the temperature of the climate in which he or she functions.

Tough-Minded Toolbox. Our strengths are our tools! This toolbox sits on the shoulders of a person, and the efficacy and effectiveness of these instruments grow in direct relationship to one's commitment to continuously searching for new strengths and their application.

Trust. The feeling that expectations will be met. The implicit belief in the integrity or strength of the potential behavior of another person.

Unity. Oneness of purpose, focus, communication and action.

Unsatisfaction. A healthy and hungry desire for new growth, new effectiveness, new levels of achievement. The reverse of dissatisfaction.

Valuability. Ability to value; ability to ascribe value to an event, circumstance, object or person and act on that value. Subjective interpretation and response—as in response-ability or responsibility.

Value. The intrinsic worth (or strength) of any person or thing. *See* Value System.

Value-Added. A product or service that has added features and benefits to delight the customer.

Value System. A dynamic, reciprocating and reinforcing conjunction of values.

Vision. A transcendent view of the possible.

Visioneering. Having vision fed by a synergistic blend of resources tooled for actual achievement. The term we use to describe the tough-minded leader's kit of tools for the future.

Vital. Bursting with life and positively directed energy.

Vulnerability. Openness to experiences. Affirmation of belief in the essential goodness and rightness of life. The absence of defensive, petty or suspicious behavior.

Warmth. Emotion and caring, flowing toward others, that transmit feelings of affirmation and reassurance.

"We" Feeling. This occurs when one particularly enjoys the practice of giving earned praise to others and when commitment to goals of the organization transcends personal wants, needs and problems. Reflected in speech by use of "we" in favor of "I." The feeling that one is part of a hard-hitting team that gets results. Ironically, this feeling is possible only when people feel like individuals—with individual purposes, values and dignity—focused on a common goal.

Wisdom. The ability or gift of transcendent vision. To see the "big picture," to visualize the immediate need or problem in proper perspective. A knowledge of fundamental truths and the ability to use them in a meaningful, developing and positive way, producing a course of action that achieves desired results.

Yeast. A volatile blend of organic substances that creates synergistic growth. The "good bacteria" are the directiveness, expedience, rigidity and other elements of style that will not meet the requirements of a turbulent tomorrow.

Family

Happily married
Get remarried annually to my wife, something I've done since 1979
Two healthy, happy, wise and well-adjusted growing daughters
My wife and I grow deeper in love, laughter and friendship
I love my children and they love me

Business

Speak professionally

Talked to over 1,000,000 people in 32 countries

Wrote or co-wrote seven bestselling books, including two *New York Times* bestsellers

Created three videos that inspired viewers

Wrote and produced 12 audio albums that helped humanity

Successfully entrepreneured seven companies

On the Board of Directors of four companies

I own my own company

To be financially free and independent

To be debt free

Health

Exercise six days a week

Enjoy and experience a totally fit body

I run, ski, skate, swim, snorkel, scuba dive, windsurf and play with my children

Keep my triglycerides and cholesterols in balance

Movies

Watch all the great movies of our time

Friendships

I have three true friends and hundreds of close acquaintances world-wide in every field

Travel

I've been around the world and enjoyed all of it. My intent is to visit all 187 countries before I die. I have visited 38 countries.

Cars

I own a Rolls Royce Silver Cloud III, a Mercedes and a Plymouth Grand Voyager

Attitudes

I am enthusiastic
positive
a possibility thinker
friendly
courteous
kind
considerate
self-confident
self reliant

Read

Two hours per day, an average of one book every other day. Admittedly some books are slim, some are skimmed and many are by close friends.

Spiritual Growth

A. Student of:
1. Dr. Robert Schuller
2. Benny Hinn
3. Dr. Peggy Bassett
4. Dr. Cherry Parker
5. Oral Roberts
6. Dr. Billy Graham
7. Ken Copeland
8. Jerry Duplantis
9. John Avanzani

B. Read the Bible from cover to cover
C. Read all the great spiritual books monthly
D. Listen to audiocassettes on the great truths

Listen

In the last 25 years, I have listened to over 10,000 audiocassettes as I drove from place to place (over 20,000 miles annually) or while exercising, either running or in a gym at least one hour daily

Create

Have an active Master Mind with Jack Canfield, Patty Hansen, Patty Aubrey, Peter Vegso and Gary Seidler
Write at least one new book per year
Complete a set of audiocassettes annually
Listen live to the 1,000 greatest speakers (I've done that and more)
Attend other people's seminars an average of 20 days per year

Visit and tour:

New York City
San Francisco
Los Angeles
San Diego
Dallas
Miami/Orlando
Chicago
Houston
Salt Lake City
Hawaii
Rome
Hong Kong
Toronto
Tokyo
Sydney/Melbourne
Perth
Bangkok
Auckland
Athens
Bombay
Calcutta
Paris
New Delhi
Canterbury

Enjoy, experience and befriend great inspiring teachers:

John Reinhardt
Dr. Buckminster Fuller

Jack Boland
Dr. Peggy Bassett
Dr. Robert Schuller
Vin Di Bono

Deliver great talks at key places (I have given over 4,500 paid presentations):

American Booksellers Association Convention
National Speakers Association
Century 21 International
National Association of Life Underwriters

I have met:

Dr. Buckminster Fuller
Hillary Rodham Clinton
Marshall McLuhan
Bob Hope
Dr. Armand Hammer
Dr. Robert Schuller
President Gerald Ford
Joel Weldon
Don Dible
Dr. Dennis Waitley
Dan Kennedy
Thea Alexander
Harvey Diamond
Dr. Billy Graham
Vin Di Bono
Chip Collins
Earl Nightengale
Dr. David Viscott
Dr. Norman Vincent Peale
General Colin Powell
Dr. Elizabeth Kubler-Ross
Og Mandino
Dr. Wayne Dyer
Cavett Robert
Zig Ziglar
Ram Dass
Jerry Gilles
Dr. Jean Houston
Jim Rohn
Dr. William Parker
Dee & Gil Stratton
Ken Keyes
John Goddard
Ira Hayes
Dr. Leo Buscaglia
Danielle Kennedy

Somers White
Bill Cosby
Peter Ueberroth
Della Reese
David Pomeranz
Pierce Brosnan
Bill Gove
Dick Gregory
Del Smith
Bryon Booth
Red Skelton
Art Linkletter
Patricia Fripp
Don Houston
Mary Kay Ash
Peter Thomas
Peter Daniels
Joe Grandolfo
Sam Curtis
Markita Andrews

JOE BATTEN'S 200 VICTORIES

Survived when born

Mastered a complex language (English) by the age of three

Learned to dress myself

Learned how to use eating utensils

Learned to respond to loving parents

Learned to get up when I fell down

Learned to give and take with other children

Learned to read

Learned to write

Learned to carry out instructions
Learned to wake up in the dark and feel calm
Learned to walk 1½ miles to and from school each day
Learned to chop wood
Learned to handle firearms
Learned to hunt effectively
Discovered the importance of risking failure in order to grow
Discovered that I was a good guy
Learned how to get up when knocked down in football and boxing
Overcame shy feelings toward girls
Made the first team in football in high school
Entered the golden gloves and won numerous matches
Set a high school record in the mile run
Made the first team in high school basketball
Enlisted in the Marines in WW II
Finished first in my platoon over the obstacle course
Survived first barroom brawl in San Diego
Came through Marine boot camp in one piece
Won three fist fights in boot camp
Discovered the logic of competing with oneself instead of one's opponent in the boxing ring
Overcame my fears in seven landings as a Marine in the South Pacific
Learned to counsel other young Marines about their fears
Won 13 boxing matches on the island of Emirau
Returned to the United States with my sanity intact
Honorable discharge from the Marine Corps
First post-war job: delivered mail in sub-zero weather
Obtained job as a tree trimmer around high-voltage power lines and survived without a shocking experience
Worked long hours in a brickyard as a laborer and was commended by employer

Sold the Veterans Administration on hiring me
Met my wife, Jean, and convinced her to marry me
Enrolled in Drake University
Averaged D the first semester—had never learned to study
Averaged C the next semester
Averaged B throughout undergraduate studies
Received all As in pursuing and obtaining a master's degree
Became an insurance agent
Mastered the selling techniques they mandated
Rebelled and quit in order to grow beyond the narrow slot in which I found myself
Obtained an entry position in Human Resources in an aircraft company
Evaluated, hired and placed hundreds of people
Represented the company in countless successful grievance hearings
Inaugurated new recruiting methods
Counseled workers on personal and work-related problems
Created unique new performance appraisal procedures
Began to learn how to really be a husband
Began to learn how to really be a father
Became training director in the aircraft company
Inaugurated first Management Information Program (MIP)
Began to make progress in eliminating stuttering
Developed new skills in writing plant-wide bulletins
Gave lectures on how to eliminate office politics
Discovered the power of prayer
Quit excessive drinking
Quit smoking
Minimized cussing and swearing
Began to learn the power of listening
Began to discover the joy of empowering others

Began to use boxing skills to teach others instead of hurting them
Learned to tell my parents I loved them
Began to understand why vulnerability is invincible
Received inspiration to leave the big corporation
Launched the company known initially as Batten & Associates
Began providing individual counseling services
Began receiving feedback on the positive results of my counsel
Obtained my first business client
Began to function as a professional consultant
Began to receive positive feedback concerning consulting matters
Acquired Leonard Hudson as a partner and colleague
We were joined by Hal Batten and Jim Swab at Batten Associates
Established new corporation known as Batten, Batten, Hudson & Swab, Inc.
Began to personally serve five clients throughout the state
Inaugurated a steady series of client innovations
Negotiated union contracts that set clients free to prosper
Provided numerous and versatile training programs
Developed a unique consulting control chart
Helped my partners begin accelerated personal and professional growth
Presented seminars for the American Management Association (AMA) throughout the U.S.
Presented seminars for AMA throughout Central America and Mexico
Targeted completing *Tough-Minded Management* in seven weeks
Completed the manuscript in seven weeks
Opened branch office in Omaha
Opened branch office in Dallas
Opened branch office in Minneapolis
Wrote *Developing a Tough-Minded Climate for Results*
Wrote *Beyond Management by Objectives*

Wrote *Dare to Live Passionately* with Leonard Hudson
Presented seminars throughout South Africa
Presented seminars throughout Canada
Presented seminars in Goose Bay, Labrador
Established Creative Media Division to produce films, videos, etc.
Established new division to present public seminars to secretaries
Expanded seminars to include 18 different subjects
We presented 750 seminars the second year
Seminar volume expanded until we were presenting over 4,000 in 1981
Awarded the Springbok Cuirasse by the Government of South Africa
Wrote *The Confidence Chasm*, co-authored with daughter, Gail
Wrote *Joe Batten's Tough-Minded Management Workbook* for BNA Communications
Wrote *Joe Batten on Sales Success*
Helped Ross Perot launch Electronic Data Systems (EDS) through his use of my books
Helped Konosuke Matsushita, through books, films, videos and audiocassettes
My books, films, videos and audiocassettes include:
Tough-Minded Leadership
Keep Reaching
When Commitments Aren't Met
Solving Employee Conflict
Power-Packed Selling: The Trust Factor in Customer Relationships
The Face-to-Face Payoff: Dynamics of the Interview
The Nuts & Bolts of Performance Appraisal
I Understand—You Understand: The Dynamics of Transactional Analysis
The ABCs of Decision Making
A Recipe for Results: Making Management by Objective Work

No-Nonsense Delegation
The Nuts & Bolts of Health Care Management Communication
Tough-Minded Interpersonal Communication for Law Enforcement
Evaluating the Performance of Law Enforcement Personnel
Creating a Tough-Minded Culture
Tough-Minded Supervision for Law Enforcement
Commitment Pays Off
Friendly Persuasion
Keep on Reaching
Trust Your Team
Dare to Dream
Tough-Minded Parenting
Ask for the Order and Get It
Your Price Is Right, Sell It
Manage Your Time to Build Your Territory
When You've Turned Down . . . Turn On
Your Sales Presentation . . . Make It a Winner
Management by Example
The Man in the Mirror
The Fully Functioning Individual
The Fully Functioning Organization
The Fully Functioning Society
How to Apply the Tough-Minded Decision-Making Process
How to Install a Tough-Minded Performance Appraisal System
Joe Batten on Management
The Greatest Secret
Face-to-Face Motivation
Face-to-Face Management
Secrets of Tough-Minded Winners
Do You Know What Time It Is?
How to Exceed Yourself
Insights & Tools

These books, films, videos and audiocassettes are helping to shape the infrastructure of several countries. They include:
Japan
Brazil
Northern Ireland
South Africa
The Kingdom of Lesotho
Received the Gold Camera Award for the film *Ask for the Order and Get It*
Awarded the CPAE, which is the equivalent of The Speaker's Hall of Fame of the National Speaker's Association
My books and seminars for the Jet Propulsion Laboratory helped launch Mariner IV to photograph the moon
Alleged by some to be one of the four leading management and leadership authorities in the world
Known as The Dean of American Sales Trainers (Dartnell)
Gave the phrase "Be all that you can be" to the U.S. Army
Developed the basic philosophy and methodology of "Build on strengths—Don't focus on weaknesses" now applied worldwide
Wrote *Expectations & Possibilities*
Wrote *Guide to Successful Living*
Wrote *Tough-Minded Leadership*
Wrote *Tough-Minded Parenting*
Wrote *Building a Total Quality Culture*

Each of the following behavioral changes was and is a victory:

FROM	TO
Role orientation	Goal orientation
Importance	Significance
Personal insecurity	Personal significance
Programs	Systems
Vague expectations	Clear expectations

Defensiveness	Open, warm, thoughtful candor
Activity focus	Progress focus
Hunch and guess	Disciplined decisions
Inconsistency	Consistency
Conformity	Individuality
Competing with others	Competing with myself
Complexity emphasis	Simplicity focus
Avoidance of problems & needs	Confrontation of problems & needs
Dialogue	Communication
Crises & firefighting	Strategic planning
Office politics	Team synergy
Blurred, expedient morality	Stretching moral standards
Focus on symptoms	Focus on causes
Diffused & disparate actions	Unity & wholeness
Compensation based on actions	Compensation based on positive performance
Fragmented thoughts & actions	Purpose & direction
Getting from others	Giving to others
Preoccupation with weaknesses	Building on strengths
Commitment to self only	Commitment to goals that transcend myself
Benign neglect	Caring & acting
Negative listening	Positive listening
Dissatisfaction	Unsatisfaction
Gamesmanship	Accountability for results
Behavioral science jargon	Tough-minded lexicon
Uncertainty	Self-confidence
Personal confusion	Viable personal faith & focus
Physical adequacy	Physical fitness
Grimness	Buoyancy
Passive personal erosion	Passionate renewal

NOTE: That's 200 and I was just getting started.
Try it—you'll like it!

Mark Victor Hansen has been called a human activator—a man who ignites individuals to recognize their full potential. During his 20-plus years as a professional speaker, he has shared his expertise in sales excellence, sales strategies, and personal empowerment and development with over one million people in 32 countries. In over 4,000 presentations, he has inspired hundreds of thousands of people to create a more powerful and purposeful future for themselves while stimulating the sale of millions of dollars worth of goods and services.

A *New York Times* bestselling author, Mark has written several books, including *Future Diary, How to Achieve Total Prosperity* and *The Miracle of Tithing.* With his best friend, Jack Canfield, Mark wrote *Chicken Soup for the Soul, A 2nd Helping of Chicken Soup for the Soul* and *Dare to Win.*

Mark believes strongly in the teaching power of audiocassettes and videocassettes. He has produced a complete library of programs that have enabled his audience members to utilize their innate abilities within their business and personal lives. His message has made him a popular radio and television personality, and he starred in his own PBS special entitled "Build a Better You."

Mark presents an annual Hawaiian retreat, "Wake Up Hawaii," designed for leaders, entrepreneurs and achievers who want to break through spiritual, mental, physical and financial blocks and unlock their highest potential. Because Mark is a strong believer in family values, this retreat includes a children's program that parallels the adult program.

Mark has dedicated his life to making a profound and positive difference in people's lives. He is a big man with a big heart and a big spirit—an inspiration to all who seek to better themselves.

For more information on Mark Victor Hansen's seminars, books and tapes, or to schedule him for a presentation to your company or organization, contact:

M. V. Hansen and Associates, Inc.
PO Box 7665
Newport Beach, CA 92658-7665

(800) 433-2314 or in California (714) 759-9304

Joe Batten, M.S., CPAE, and head of Joe Batten Associates, has spoken to over 80 percent of the Fortune 500 companies, as well as to hundred of young, start-up companies and many major associations. He is often introduced as "one of the five leading business consultants in the world."

Joe is the author of 16 books, 35 training films and videos, and scores of audio programs, including *The Greatest Secret.* Among his books are *Tough-Minded Leadership* (AMACOM, 1989), *Expectations and Possibilities* (Hay House, 1990) and *Tough-Minded Parenting* (Broadman, 1991). *Tough-Minded Leadership* was voted Book of the Year by the American Management Association and is a bestseller. His most recent book prior to *The Master Motivator* is *Building a Total Quality Culture* (Crisp, 1992). *Total Quality Leadership* will follow *The Master Motivator.* Joe has just finished taping two new 20-minute videos with Ross Perot titled *Perot and Batten on Leadership.* They will be accompanied by an audiocassette album and a book of the same name.

Among the large corporations for whom Batten has provided training and consultant services are Xerox, IBM, McDonald's, ServiceMaster, Hospital Corporation of America, General Motors, Exxon, Ford and American Bankers Association. He provided the U.S. Defense Department with the phrase, "Be All That You Can Be."

Batten has been a keynote speaker, held seminars and conducted workshops for over 50 major universities, including MIT, Cal Tech, Texas A&M, Duquesne, San Diego State, the Universities of Ottawa, California, Michigan, Wisconsin, British Columbia, and Ulster in Northern Ireland.

Batten is a speaker, trainer and mentor who:

- has keynoted more international conferences than any other American
- has spoken over 3,000 times throughout the world

- was one of the first ten people inducted into the Speakers Hall of Fame
- wrote the bestselling book *Tough-Minded Management,* now translated into 21 languages
- has been interviewed on radio and TV over 500 times on his unique "tough-minded" and "building on strengths" messages
- is often referred to as The Dean of American Sales Trainers

The cultures of literally thousands of organizations throughout the world are outgrowths of the "tough-minded" books authored by Joe Batten, beginning with *Tough-Minded Management,* first published in 1963 and called "the greatest management book ever" by Ross Perot. Konosuke Matsushita, the late chairman of the Matsushita Corporation, referred to the book as his "secular bible."

In addition to speaking, writing and training, Joe's forte is *mentoring* and *coaching* leaders and potential leaders at all levels. Joe can be contacted at:

Joe Batten
Joe Batten Associates
4505 S.W. 26th Street
Des Moines, IA 50321
phone & fax (515) 285-8069